D1239633

Images

Titles in the Resource Books for Teachers series

Beginners
Peter Grundy

Classroom Dynamics
Jill Hadfield

Conversation
Rob Nolasco and Lois Arthur

Creative Poetry Writing
Jane Spiro

Cultural Awareness
Barry Tomalin and Susan Stempleski

Dictionaries
Jon Wright

Drama
Charlyn Wessels

Drama and Improvisation
Ken Wilson

English for Specific Purposes
Keith Harding

Exam Classes
Peter May

Film
Susan Stempleski and Barry Tomalin

Global Issues
Ricardo Sampedro and Susan Hillyard

Grammar
Scott Thornbury

Grammar Dictation
Ruth Wajnryb

Homework
Lesley Painter

The Internet
Scott Windeatt, David Hardisty,
and D. Eastment

Learner-based Teaching
Colin Campbell and Hanna Kryszewska

Letters
Nicky Burbidge, Peta Gray, Sheila Levy,
and Mario Rinvolucri

Listening
Goodith White

Literature
Alan Duff and Alan Maley

Music and Song
Tim Murphey

Newspapers
Peter Grundy

Project Work 2nd edition
Diana L. Fried-Booth

Pronunciation
Clement Laroy

Role Play
Gillian Porter Ladousse

Storybuilding
Jane Spiro

**Teaching Other Subjects
Through English**
Sheelagh Deller and Chris Price

Teenagers
Gordon Lewis

Vocabulary 2nd edition
John Morgan and Mario Rinvolucri

Writing 2nd edition
Tricia Hedge

Primary Resource Books

Art and Crafts with Children
Andrew Wright

Assessing Young Learners
Sophie Ioannou-Georgiou
and Pavlos Pavlou

Creating Chants and Songs
Carolyn Graham

Creating Stories with Children
Andrew Wright

Drama with Children
Sarah Phillips

Games for Children
Gordon Lewis with Günther Bedson

Grammar for Young Learners
Gordon Lewis and Hans Mol

The Internet and Young Learners
Gordon Lewis

Projects with Young Learners
Diane Phillips, Sarah Burwood,
and Helen Dunford

Storytelling with Children
Andrew Wright

Very Young Learners
Vanessa Reilly and Sheila M. Ward

Writing with Children
Jackie Reilly and Vanessa Reilly

Young Learners
Sarah Phillips

Resource Books for Teachers

series editor Alan Maley

Images

Jamie Keddie

OXFORD

UNIVERSITY PRESS

OXFORD
UNIVERSITY PRESS

Great Clarendon Street, Oxford OX2 6DP

Oxford University Press is a department of the University of Oxford.
It furthers the University's objective of excellence in research, scholarship,
and education by publishing worldwide in

Oxford New York

Auckland Cape Town Dar es Salaam Hong Kong Karachi
Kuala Lumpur Madrid Melbourne Mexico City Nairobi
New Delhi Shanghai Taipei Toronto

With offices in

Argentina Austria Brazil Chile Czech Republic France Greece
Guatemala Hungary Italy Japan Poland Portugal Singapore
South Korea Switzerland Thailand Turkey Ukraine Vietnam

OXFORD and OXFORD ENGLISH are registered trade marks of
Oxford University Press in the UK and in certain other countries

© Oxford University Press 2009

The moral rights of the author have been asserted

Database right Oxford University Press (maker)

First published 2009

2013 2012 2011 2010
10 9 8 7 6 5 4 3 2

All rights reserved. No part of this publication may be reproduced, stored in
a retrieval system, or transmitted, in any form or by any means, without the
prior permission in writing of Oxford University Press (with the sole exception
of photocopying carried out under the conditions stated in the paragraph
headed 'Photocopying'), or as expressly permitted by law, or under terms
agreed with the appropriate reprographics rights organization. Enquiries
concerning reproduction outside the scope of the above should be sent to the
ELT Rights Department, Oxford University Press, at the address above

You must not circulate this book in any other binding or cover
and you must impose this same condition on any acquirer

Photocopying

The Publisher grants permission for the photocopying of those pages marked
'photocopiable' according to the following conditions. Individual purchasers
may make copies for their own use or for use by classes that they teach. School
purchasers may make copies for use by staff and students, but this permission
does not extend to additional schools or branches

Under no circumstances may any part of this book be photocopied for resale

Any websites referred to in this publication are in the public domain and their
addresses are provided by Oxford University Press for information only. Oxford
University Press disclaims any responsibility for the content

ISBN: 978 0 19 442579 7

Printed in China

This book is printed on paper from certified and well-managed sources.

Acknowledgements

The author would like to thank the following people: photographer Annick Wolfers for invaluable support and advice on all fronts; Roger Hunt for guidance; Gerard, Daniel and Stephanie for being inspirational fellow teachers; Nick Southey and Susie Keddie for all their valuable feedback; Alan Maley and Julia Sallabank for giving me my first break; editor Helen Forrest and art editor Donna Thynne for all their hard work and dedication to this project; visual Communications educator Paul Martin Lester for inspiration; illustrator Nicolás Antonio Dionis Álvarez for a great job; Jennifer and everyone else at *The English House*, Seville for being so understanding; artist Jo Wray for his photograph; my artistic students for all their illustrations used in chapters 1 and 6 (not forgetting Barbara, Gemma, Yolanda, Chus, Lauren, Tom, Puri, Georgina, Pep and Roser whose names do not appear on the pictures on pages 19 and 119); my photogenic students (Daniela, Delia, Elena, Gloria, Graziella, Maria Grazia, Marta, Monica, Roberto, Rossella, Santina and Teresa) for their pictures in chapter 4; all my long running students for their patience, inspiration and friendship: Dimpna, Arnau, Coral, Miquel, Roser, Pep, Puri, Marta, Helena, Eva, Itziar, Núria, Ricard, Oscar, Roser, Chus, Àngels, Gloria, Felipe, Maribel, Manel and Sara to name a few; my family (Richard, Anne, Jack, Susie and Alastair) for all their love and support.

For Richard Cassidy (my grandfather)

The authors and publishers are grateful to those who have given permission to reproduce the following extracts and adaptations of copyright material:

p108 'The Best' (Holly Knight / Mike Chapman). ©1988 Knighty Knight Music and Primary Wave Knight (Administered by Wixen Music Publishing, Inc.) and Mike Chapman Publishing Enterprises Licensed courtesy of Finchley Music Publishing Ltd and Mike Chapman Publishing Enterprises.

Sources:

p 31 http://www.munch.museum.no

p 52 New York Exposed by Sean O'Sullivan

p 79 Inward Vision (1958), Creative Credo (1920) (Paul Klee quote)

The publisher would like to thank the following for their permission to reproduce photographs and other copyright material:

Cover photograph courtesy Bert Hardy/Hulton Archive/Getty Images.

Alamy p 98 (pony tail/André Schuster, cat walk/Gari Wyn Williams), 102 (greyhounds/Avico Ltd), 105 (Elvis Presley/Mary Evans Picture Library), 105 (ET/Movie Magic, CD/Sciencephotos); Advertising Archives p 44; Artist Partners and David Frankland p 101 (cover of *Frozen in Time*); Associated Press p 107 (Robert Wadlow and family); Corbis pp 22(Hinderburg/Bettmann), 28 (*Las Meninas* by Diego Velazquez/Bettmann), 33 (Buzz Aldrin), 42 (lions/Tom Brakefield), 46 (naughty dog/Lawrence Mannin/Corbis), 81 (Govinda/Sherwin Crato/ Reuters), 85 (House boat/SUPRI/Reuters), 101 (David Kennedy plays the didgeridoo/Paul A Sounders); DACS p78 (*The Physical Impossibility of Death in the Mind of the Living* by kind permission of Damien Hirst); Daily News Photos New York pp 51 and 65 (Edna Egbert/Charles Payne); Getty Images pp 15 (panda/Bert Hardy/Hulton Archive), 26 (baby gorilla/Grey Villet/Time Life Pictures), 48 (stealing the *Scream*/AFP), 60 (Japanese wedding/Yoshikazu Tsuno/AFP), 71 (Queen Elizabeth II, Tony Blair/Anwar Hussein), 73 (Amundsen/Illustrated London News/ Hulton Archive), 88 (Olympic Games Poster); Guinness World Records p 63 (fingernails, milk balancing, rattle snakes/Drew Gardner); Image Quest Marine p 90 (swimming elephant/Jeff Yonover); iStockPhoto pp 67 (clock, 81, speed limit/iStockPhoto/135/Luis Carlos Torres), 87 (Olympic icons), 95 (Anthony Berenyi/digital watch), 104 (kissing fish/Miodrag Gajic); Jamie Keddie pp 58 (*Botero's Cat*), 69 (dirty dog), 82 (Roberto Manzoni/tired and exhausted, Elena Carugati/bored, Graziella Saccoccio/relaxed, Marta Omincini/confused, Santina Suriano/disappointed, Monica Santus/Embarrassed, Rossella Bettoni/ frightened, Maria G Consonni/annoyed) p 83 (Elena Carugati/bored); Kobal Collection pp 49 (*The Brain Eaters*); 75 (*Dr Strangelove*); Magnum pp 52 and 65 (Café Flore/Dennis Stock); OUP pp 21 (map/Clip Art), 73 (Union Jack), 95 (gold watch, stopwatch/Photodisc, Ladies watch with black face, child's watch, gent's gold watch, silver watches, gent's waterproof watch), 98 (traffic jam/Photodisc, couch potato/Digital Vision, light house/Photodisc, sun flower/Photodisc), 102 (New York/ Photodisc, hotdog), 104 (lipstick/Stokbyte), 105 (breakfast in bed/ Photodisc); Rex Features pp 34 (Patty Hearst); Time Inc p 37 (Time cover Sept 29 1975); Jo Wray p 54 (*Upside Down Tree People*).

Illustrations by: Nicolás Antonio Dionis Álvarez pp 18 (Romeo and Juliet), 40 (elephant in a fridge). pp 8 (hamburger) 19 (fishermen) and flashcards pp 113, 114, and 119 c/o the author.

Contents

Activity	Level	Time (minutes)	Aims	

Section II Productive skills

3 Writing

4 Speaking

The author and series editor

Jamie Keddie is a Barcelona-based teacher, teacher trainer, and writer. He previously worked as a biochemist and then as a musician before moving into language teaching in 2001 and setting up a small business specializing in providing English classes for professionals.

In 2008, he founded TEFLclips.com, a site dedicated to the possibilities for online video-sharing in the classroom. He is the author of many articles on a number of subjects including the use of corpora in language learning. He is a keen conference speaker.

Alan Maley worked for the British Council from 1966 to 1988, serving as English Language Officer in Yugoslavia, Ghana, Italy, France, and China, and as Regional Representative in South India (Madras). From 1988 to 1993, he was Director-General of the Bell Educational Trust, Cambridge. From 1993 to 1998 he was Senior Fellow in the Department of English Language and Literature of the National University of Singapore, and from 1998 to 2003 he was Director of the graduate programme at Assumption University, Bangkok. He is currently a freelance consultant. Among his publications are *Literature* (in this series), *Beyond Words, Sounds Interesting, Sounds Intriguing, Words, Variations on a Theme*, and *Drama Techniques in Language Learning* (all with Alan Duff), *The Mind's Eye* (with Françoise Grellet and Alan Duff), *Learning to Listen* and *Poem into Poem* (with Sandra Moulding), *Short and Sweet*, and *The Language Teacher's Voice*.

Foreword

The power of visual imagery to convey messages, to send affective signals and to stimulate the imagination is well attested. There are indeed already a number of books on language teaching which have tapped into this rich vein. There are however, at least two reasons for looking anew at the use of still images. On the one hand, we are now submerged in a flood of moving images, which tends to distract us from giving concentrated attention to one or more still pictures. On the other, we now have available infinite resources for accessing, storing, and retrieving digitally generated images. Yet so far, this rich resource has been relatively poorly understood or exploited.

This book addresses both these issues. It is noteworthy for the exceptional quality of the images presented, some of them historically iconic. They are striking, affectively engaging and memorable. This aids the process of paying real detailed attention to an image. The ideas for utilizing the images in the teaching of a foreign language are similarly striking and original, whether they are used to illustrate or present language points, to offer systematic practice, or to stimulate creative and imaginative spin-off.

Throughout, the author has been at pains to suggest simple yet effective ways of using currently available technology to enrich the visual landscape of the classroom, through image search engines, image sharing, image manipulation applications and the like. This will prove highly useful for any teacher using the book. The approach to technology is uncomplicated and non-threatening, so that even technologically challenged teachers will find it accessible.

The author has also emphasized the importance of involving learners in resourcing visual materials for themselves and for use in class, including the important role of student-made visuals. This is particularly significant in an age when our students are likely to be more familiar with the latest technology than their teachers. A whole chapter of the book is devoted to this.

There are also extensive references to banks of visual images which will facilitate access to a wide range of visual materials.

The book offers a refreshing approach to the uses of a resource which is so familiar to teachers that they may have taken it for granted, and perhaps even overlooked the power and the impact such materials can have.

Alan Maley

Introduction

The story of Robert Pershing Wadlow is a sad one. He loved photography, stamp collecting, and his family, and although you may not be aware of his name, I am sure you would recognize him instantly if you were to see a photograph. My favourite one is a family snap, taken in a garden somewhere in Midwest USA shortly before 1940. Mum, dad, brothers, and sisters smile as they stand lined up for the camera. Robert stands behind them all, his left hand resting on his father's shoulder and his right hand on his brother Eugene's. As I look at Robert and his graceful smile, I try to imagine what his life was like and how he must have suffered as he wished he could join his family in the foreground of the picture like any normal boy. Robert died when he was 22 years old and 2.72 metres tall. He is the tallest man in medical history.

Images speak to us. They give rise to outbursts of emotion, thought, and curiosity. They bring back memories and remind us of the experiences we have had. Image refreshes the parts of the brain that words alone fail to reach.

In this book, we will see how all of this image-induced mind activity can be channelled into language and communication in a learning situation.

Aims

The book has 5 aims:

1 to examine the huge number of possibilities and reasons for using non-moving images and pictures in the language classroom
2 to suggest categories of image that can be used, where they can be obtained, how they can be displayed, and how they can be stored
3 to inspire teachers to look out for engaging images and create their own activities around them
4 to demonstrate how virtually any pre-existing text-based activity can be strengthened and improved with an aspect of image
5 to present a bank of diverse, original, and practical teaching ideas that involve images, the majority of which will not require a great deal of preparation.

Who this book is for

The book has been written for:

- all practising teachers of English as a foreign or second language
- teachers involved in the education of other languages. Despite the fact that the book's emphasis is on English language teaching, nearly all of the activities can be adapted for the teaching of other languages.
- trainee language teachers
- teacher trainers and course organizers
- any teacher who wishes to investigate ways of using images as a basis for classwork (group conversations, for example).

The book makes no assumptions regarding readers' teaching experience, background, or knowledge.

Reasons for using images

What follows are some thoughts (presented in no particular order) that advocate the strength of images as a language learning resource.

A perfect marriage

It is said that if you tell someone about your dreams, you are more likely to remember them. The principle may be the same in a language learning situation: when we combine words with images, the whole learning experience may become more memorable and productive.

Words and images are inseparable. We read or hear words and think of images. We see images and think of words. If we merely focus on one over the other, we will inevitably miss out on the full picture and in turn overlook learning and teaching opportunities.

Any mentally stimulating image will require language to qualify it. Consider the millions of words that must have been spoken or written about Picasso's *Guernica*, or the fact that it is not uncommon practice for a journalist to be presented with an image and asked to write a story around it.

Thus many of the activities in this book demonstrate either how language can be extracted from an image or how a picture can be constructed from a text.

Engagement

Many teachers will be aware of the disappointing situation in which a carefully selected article or other text fails to give rise to the class discussion that was hoped or predicted. We may consider what we did wrong: Did we fail to pre-teach the necessary vocabulary? Perhaps we got the skimming and scanning activities the wrong way around? Did we ask the right questions? The truth is, however, that conversations aren't naturally born through such procedures.

To get to the root of the problem, it is necessary to ask ourselves what we really want to achieve with the material that we take into the classroom. Although an imported text may provide learners with a model or 'template' for language production, it is incorrect to assume that it will necessarily provide them with a *reason*.

If our objective is to get our learners speaking or writing, we may want to take a leaf out of Stuart Ewen's book. In *All Consuming Images*, he writes: '… if you really want to move people, don't use words, use images.'

The activities in this book aim to demonstrate how images may be used to engage, stir up curiosity, provide inspiration and motivation for writing and speaking, and generally enhance learners' classroom experience.

Language voids and information gaps

Whereas a text supplies the language explicitly, an image *implies* it and thus creates a void to be filled.

What does this mean? Well, imagine that you are teaching a group of five students and you show them Sam Shere's famous photograph of the Hindenburg disaster (Activity 1.5, page 22). Despite the fact that all of your learners may have seen the image before, none of them was alive when the event took place. Naturally, knowledge of it varies from learner to learner. If we are to represent the situation with a graph, it might look something like this

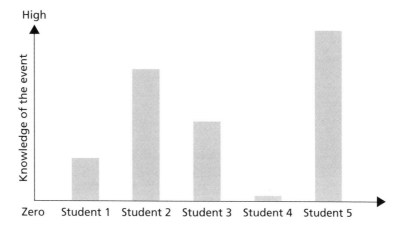

The potential of the image in question, then, is firstly to engage learners with the event, secondly to give rise to natural information gaps (such as the one between Student 4 and Student 5, for example), and thirdly to expose a void which must be filled with words.

Meaning

If you have read the *Harry Potter* books in Spanish, you will know that he has a pet *lechuza*. Look this word up in a Spanish dictionary and you will find that it means *owl*. Imagine that you are studying Spanish and you have already learned that the word for owl is *búho*. You ask your teacher to explain the difference and she does (in Spanish of course). The explanation goes right over your head but in order to avoid embarrassment, you nod to signal that you have understood.

What your teacher has effectively just done is to describe two images: her mental image for a *lechuza* and her mental image for a *búho*. Now, imagine that instead of describing these images to you, she actually goes one further and shows them to you. She types the two words into an Internet image search engine and you instantly *see* the difference: A *lechuza* is a barn owl and a *búho* is a tawny or long-eared owl.

If we are to conclude that image is an important factor for understanding the meaning of a piece of language, we are grossly underestimating its importance. Image *is* meaning.

It may be worth pointing out that we are not limiting ourselves to the use of image to 'explain' individual words. A grammatical structure, a sentence, or even a whole newspaper article can potentially be defined by a single image. If we introduce learners to any piece of language via its image, we start with meaning first.

I paid for the hamburger

I paid the hamburger

Agency

Upon being presented with a number of different images or pictures, an individual may need only a moment to identify one that he or she connects with. Many of the activities in this book exploit this feature in an attempt to give learners a choice in the tasks and assignments that are involved.

If we give our learners a say in the content of a lesson, we increase the possibility that they will engage with it. This in turn can lead to optimized learning results. Similarly, if students are allowed to choose from a number of different homework assignments, the chances of successful homework accomplishment may be improved. In pedagogical terms, learner choice or involvement in class content is referred to as 'agency'. As we will see, activities which involve multiple images are effective in providing agency.

Memory and language reactivation

From a simplified psychological point of view, let us imagine that a word, or other discrete item of language, is a tiny hub positioned somewhere in the human brain. Via the spokes that extend from it, the hub is connected to many other pieces of information. Schematically, it might look something like this:

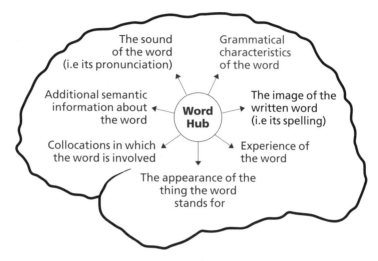

Now let us imagine that whenever a learner is introduced to a new word or piece of language, a new hub will emerge in his or her head. As a general rule, the more memorable that experience, the stronger the hub's resulting foundations will be.

The experience of meeting new language will surely be heightened for most if it is accompanied by memorable and engaging pictures, diagrams, and images. Chapter 6, for example, presents a number of activities in which the learner experiences new language by drawing it.

From that point onwards, it should be the aim and responsibility for both learner and teacher alike to strengthen spokes and cultivate new ones—an essential process if the target language is to be promoted to the learner's active vocabulary. This can be done only through subsequent multiple meetings of the target language and this, in turn, takes us to one of the most important uses for image in the classroom.

An image can be used at later dates to access any language that was learned in conjunction with it. In this way, it provides the teacher with an invaluable tool for recalling, retrieving, revising, recapping, and reactivating target language.

Technology and the image age

We are currently living in the age of the mediated image. Recent advances in information technology, digital photography, and printing processes have consolidated the role of image as a highly effective medium of communication.

Perhaps as a result of this, many of us claim to be visual thinkers and this in turn may affect our learning approaches. As a teaching resource, authentic image-based materials have never been so easy to acquire, and when they are integrated into the classroom the resulting environment will come to resemble the real world.

For the technologically orientated classroom, images can be digitally obtained, stored and, displayed. Teachers and learners may decide to take advantage of the current influx of popular image technologies and phenomena such as digital cameras, image search engines, image sharing, image organizers, image manipulation applications, video-editing software, video-sharing sites, and more.

Convenience

When we use an image in class, we are not necessarily bound to make photocopies of it for everyone. As a result, it may be possible to carry around a large number of lessons and activities in a single folder or a few thousand images on a single gigabyte.

An international 'language'

In an attempt to avoid learner confusion, a teacher may decide to adapt or alter a text that is to be used in the classroom. Images, on the other hand, work best when they are authentic. Visual communication can potentially surpass boundaries that a given spoken language cannot, and, importantly for the language classroom, the subjective process of interpretation may work best as a dialogic, collaborative effort.

Furthermore, if activities are planned around images rather than texts, the language teacher working abroad will be able to benefit from the local media as a useful resource (often a lot more economical than having to buy magazines and newspapers in English).

Content and language integration

From the moment we are born, we are subjected to an onslaught of visual messages. Among those who attempt to reach out to us are advertisers, governments, journalists, and those who work in public relations. For years they have been aware of the effectiveness of image as a tool for sculpting public opinion and behaviour.

Only the most naïve individual would assume that their motives are always good and, in such a climate, the need for rational thought is always upon us. According to visual communications educator, Paul Martin Lester, 'The goal of education is to teach an individual how to seek factual information and base reasoned conclusions on those data.'

Just like words, images have a grammar of their own—a set of rules for processing and analysing them. The study of these rules will combine, among many other things, elements of psychology, graphic design (the importance of colour, form, depth, and movement for example), photography, semiotics, journalism, advertising, public relations, stereotyping, and ethics.

Many of the activities on a visual communication (or visual literacy) course will be highly communicative. This is due to the fact that any task which involves image analysis may work best as a collaborative effort in which individuals share and discuss different ideas. For this reason, it is an excellent area to integrate into the language classroom.

Of course, there are other image-based subjects that can be integrated into the language class besides: art, design, cinematography, photography, media studies, etc.

How to use this book

How the book is organized

The main part of the book consists of a bank of diverse activities and practical teaching ideas, all of which involve an aspect of image. These are divided into six chapters over three sections.

Section I Receptive skills

This section looks at ways in which an element of image may be incorporated into the listening and reading activities that we prepare for our learners. There may be many reasons for doing so.

- An image may stir up curiosity and motivate a learner to read or listen to a complementing text. For this reason, teachers may choose to use the stories behind images of people, pieces of art, famous photographs, personal photographs, or even album covers as the basis for reading or listening activities.
- When a learner is given access to an image that complements a listening or reading activity, his or her comprehension of the text may be reinforced.
- By studying texts which describe images, learners may be equipped with language that is vital for a wide range of diverse situations.
- An image may be used at later dates to refresh, revisit, and revise the language that was studied in conjunction with it.

Chapter 1 includes ideas for incorporating image into listening activities; Chapter 2 has ideas for visually enhancing reading activities.

Section II Productive skills

Language cannot be produced without thought. An image may spark the imagination, awaken memories, uncover issues, and much more. This section looks at ways in which images may unlock language in learners' minds and be used as the basis for diverse writing and speaking activities.

Chapter 3 considers how images may be used to provide reason and motivation to write; Chapter 4 explores how to encourage speaking and conversation through the use of images.

Section III Grammar and vocabulary

This section explores how series of images may be used to elicit, teach, drill, and revise the vocabulary, idioms, and grammar that our learners require and request.

Chapter 5 sees an old favourite teaching aid—the traditional picture flashcard—undergoing a technological makeover. Meanwhile, Chapter 6 addresses some novel uses for a more established piece of technology—the pencil.

Appendix

The Appendix offers a lot of supplementary information that will be useful in conjunction with the activities.

How each activity is organized

A good chef will never follow a recipe step-by-step, exactly as it is laid out in the book. It is more likely that he or she will take inspiration from it and adapt it according to personal taste and style. The same idea should apply to teachers and lesson plans.

The activities that are offered in the main section of the book are accompanied by the following information.

Level:	This is the minimum proficiency level with which the activity can be carried out. With a little thought, however, most of the activities can be adapted for lower levels.
Time:	A rough indication of how long the activity will last. Since good images can give rise to spontaneous, unplanned discussion, there is no way of knowing exactly how long an activity will take.
Aims:	A mention of the language points or skills that the activity addresses.
Preparation:	A description of the materials you will need for the activity and how to prepare.
Procedure:	The step-by-step guide to the activity.
Variation:	In many cases, variations are suggested.
Follow-up:	Follow-up activities or homework assignments are often suggested.

A note about the images in the book

Many of the images in this book have been included primarily to give teachers an idea of the type that would work well for certain activities. In other cases, teachers will want to take advantage of the specific images that are on offer. This will usually involve holding up the book for students to see. At times, it will be necessary to cover up and hide other elements on the page (i.e. pieces of text and other images) that may spoil subsequent steps of the activity.

It is worth pointing out that as a result of the author's background and teaching experience, many of the images referred to in this book are rooted in western history, culture, and media. Consequently, learners will almost certainly have varying attitudes and connections with them.

At times, it may be advantageous to encourage learners to seek out images from their own lives, backgrounds, and cultures, and bring these into class. Teachers can then consider how activities may be planned around them.

1
Listening

The first two activities in this chapter demonstrate how words can be used to construct images in students' minds. Unlike a standard picture dictation in which students draw a picture that is described to them, in these activities the brain itself is the canvas and any attempt to recreate the image will require a reconstruction of the text. The remaining activities start with images before moving on to the counterpart texts that provide stories or descriptions.

1.1 Mental picture dictation

Level Elementary +

Time 30 minutes

Aims To listen to the description of an image in order to visualize it.

Preparation

Select an engaging image and prepare a short description of it.

Example *This is a black and white photograph that was taken in 1939 at London Zoo. We see a young Chinese photographer called Ming taking a photograph of his friend Mike, a little English boy. Mike is on the right hand side of the photograph. He is sitting on a chair wearing black shorts and a long-sleeved T-shirt with a collar. Ming is on the left. His camera is on a tripod but since Ming is not very tall, he is standing on a chair to reach it.*

Procedure

1 Tell your students that you are going to describe an interesting picture.

2 Describe the picture without letting your students see it (it is important they don't realize that one of the protagonists is a panda). Explain any unknown words as you go along (using gesture, for example) and write these up on the board.

3 Repeat the description a second time and ask your students if they understand everything you have said. Be aware that some students may misunderstand the description and think that Ming took the photograph that you are describing. This presents a logical problem—how could he take the photograph and be in it at the same time? You may need to repeat the description a few more times during steps 4, 5, and 6 (below).

4 Put your students into pairs or small groups and ask them to write out the full description of the picture as accurately as possible from memory.

5 Allow pairs or groups to merge and compare what they have written with each other. Allow them to make changes to their texts if they like.

6 Conduct a feedback—nominate students to relay the picture descriptions back to you as they have written them. Encourage peer error correction when possible and offer help when necessary.

7 Write your own description on the board and allow your students to copy it and compare it with their own.

8 Ask your students if they would like to see the photograph. Tell them that when they see it, they will get a surprise and ask them to guess why this might be. This can be an opportunity to work with question forms. If you want to give a clue, tell your students that Ming is also wearing a collar but a different type to the one Mike is wearing.

9 Show your students the picture.

Variation 1

Instead of asking your students to write the description at step 4, ask for a volunteer to come up to the board. Let him or her rewrite the entire description with the help and support of the other students. This technique takes all the attention away from the teacher and gives your students the opportunity to work on the text independently as a group.

Variation 2

There are a number of ways in which image descriptions could be generated by students themselves. One way to do this would be to divide the class into two groups and show one image to group A and another image to group B. Have everyone prepare a description of their image before pairing up members from group A with members from group B and asking them to dictate their images to each other.

Comment

The boy in the photograph is Michael Hardy, photographer Bert Hardy's son.

1.2 Running dictation: Romeo and Juliet

Level   Elementary +

Time   25 minutes

Aims   To listen to the description of an image in preparation for a lateral thinking activity.

Preparation

In a running dictation, students are put into small groups at one end of the classroom and a text is put on the classroom wall at the other end. Each group nominates a 'runner' whose job is to make repeated journeys to the text and memorize sections of it which are brought back to the other members and dictated to them verbatim. In preparation for this activity, make a copy of the text below and attach it to the board or one of the classroom walls (for large groups, use two or three copies on different parts of the wall to avoid overcrowding). If you have a small classroom, you may prefer to take your students outside for this activity.

Foul play?

Romeo and Juliet are dead. They are lying on the floor in a bedroom. The floor is very wet. Romeo and Juliet are surrounded by lots of pieces of broken glass. There is a shelf above them. There is no one in the house. All the windows and doors are locked and there is no sign of a break-in. The house is situated in a remote location very close to a railway track. Can you explain what happened?

Photocopiable © Oxford University Press

Procedure

1   Tell your students that you have a puzzle for them about two lovers called Romeo and Juliet. Show them the text on the wall.

2   Divide your students into groups and position them as far away from the text on the wall as possible. Ask each group to nominate a runner. Everyone else will need a pencil and paper.

3   When you give the signal, runners have to make repeated journeys between their groups and the text. On each trip, the runner should attempt to remember a chunk of language and then relay it to his or her group members who write it down.

4   Once the task has been completed, allow students to correct their work by comparing it with the text on the wall.

5 Explain any words or terms that students don't understand in the text before putting them into pairs or small groups to work on the puzzle.

6 Allow each group to share their theories with the rest of the class.

7 Allow students to ask you questions about the puzzle.

8 When students either solve the puzzle or give up on it, show them the image below.

9 Make sure everyone understands that Romeo and Juliet are goldfish and their bowl fell off the shelf because of the vibrations of a passing train.

Variation

With a less energetic class, dictate the text to your students in the normal way.

Comment

Running dictations are naturally competitive and it is a good idea to take the precaution of moving as many potentially dangerous pieces of furniture and other objects out of the way. A good friend of mine tells me that he once had a student sprain her ankle during a running dictation. You have been warned!

1.3 Drawing a song

Level Elementary +

Time 20 minutes

Aims To engage with a song by drawing key language from the lyrics before listening.

Preparation

For this activity, you should choose a song with good descriptive elements or scenes that you can ask your students to draw before playing it to them. The drawing process should both engage students with the lyrics, and activate vocabulary that is central to comprehension. Suitable songs would be *California Dreaming*, *Raining in my Heart*, *Summertime*, *Message in a Bottle*, or *My Favourite Things*. The procedure outlined here shows how to use a song that is usually associated with children but often popular with adults.

Procedure

1 Give your students the following instructions:

I want you to draw three pictures: In the first picture, I want you to draw a fisherman or a fisherwoman. In the second picture, he or she has caught a fish. In the third picture he or she has decided to let the fish go.

2 Ask your students to repeat the instructions back to you before drawing.

3 Elicit as many reasons as possible why the fisherman or fisherwoman decided to let the fish go and write these on the board. At some stage suggest that the fish bit his or her finger and add this to the list.

4 Teach your students the following song:

| One | two | | three | four | five | | Once I | caught a | | fish | a – live |

| Six, | sev – en, | | eight | nine | ten | | Then I | let it | | go | a – gain |

| Why | did | you | let | him | go? | | Be – cause it | bit | my | fin – ger | so |

| Which | fin – ger | | did | it | bite? | | This lit – tle | fin – ger | | on | my right |

5 Put the song lyrics up on the classroom wall beside your students' artwork. The lyrics contain two past simple question forms that may be referred to whenever the need arises at later dates.

Comment

Many students and teachers will feel self-conscious about singing in class. One way to deal with this would be to chant the song rather than sing it. Chanting is an effective way of practising pronunciation (especially stress patterns), memorizing pieces of language and internalizing grammar structures.

1.4 Dictated sentences

Level Elementary to intermediate

Time 30 minutes

Aims To listen to a number of sentences that describe a picture.

Preparation

Prepare approximately 10–12 sentences that relate to a picture, some of which are true and some of which are false. For example, if we were using a map of Europe, we could say:

Example *Bulgaria is directly south of Romania.* (true)
Vilnius is in Lithuania. (true)
Minsk is in Ukraine. (false)
Poland has a bigger land mass than Hungary. (true)
The North Sea is between Sweden and Finland. (false)
Latvia is north of Lithuania. (true)
Portugal is longer than Italy. (false)
Luxembourg has borders with Belgium, France, and Germany. (true)
Slovakia is west of Austria. (false)
Poland doesn't have a coast line. (false)
Some people say that Italy looks like a boot. (true)
Norway is east of Sweden. (false)

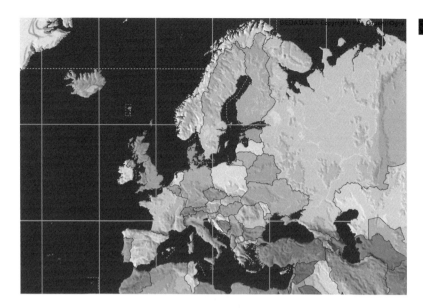

Procedure

1 Tell your students that you are going to give them an observation test and let them study the map (or other picture) for two or three minutes.

2 Remove the picture from your students' sight and tell them that you have a number of sentences that relate to it, some of which are true and some false.

3 Dictate the sentences to your students. During the dictation, if a student thinks that a statement is true, he or she should write it exactly as you say it. If on the other hand the student thinks that it is false, he or she should amend it accordingly.

Example *Teacher says:*   *Portugal is longer than Italy.*
Students could write: Portugal is not longer than Italy.
              Italy is longer than Portugal.
              Portugal is about the same size as Italy.

4 Once all statements have been dictated, allow everyone to compare what they wrote.

5 Show your students the sentences you dictated and let them see the picture again.

Variation 1

At step 5, set up an information gap by giving only one student access to the picture and asking others to ask questions about it. This will involve converting the true and false sentences into questions.

Variation 2

Create true and false statements about an image that your learners know very well—a picture from the classroom wall, for example. Remove the picture and when students enter the classroom, ask them if they notice anything different about the place. After establishing that a picture is missing, dictate the true and false questions using the past tense.

Variation 3

Take a group photograph of your students and before the next class, prepare true and false sentences that describe what individuals were wearing.

Follow-up

Using the sentences that you created as a model, ask your students to make their own true and false statements: Choose two images, divide the class into two groups, and give one image to group A and the other to group B. Briefly let group A see group B's image and vice versa. Finally pair up students from group A with students from group B and allow them to test each other's powers of observation as before.

1.5 Dictogloss

Level Intermediate +

Time 40 minutes

Aims To listen to the story behind a picture and then reconstruct the text from memory.

Preparation

Select any picture which has an interesting story behind it (a historic photograph, for example) and prepare a short text that summarizes the facts that relate to it. For example:

The Hindenburg disaster

The Hindenburg Zeppelin was a masterpiece of German engineering. At 245 metres long, it still holds the record as being the largest aircraft ever built. On the 6th May, 1937, the airship was about to complete its first transatlantic passenger flight of the year to the USA. While landing at Lakehurst Naval Air Station, New Jersey, disaster struck. Above a crowd which included many journalists and photographers, the Hindenburg burst into flames and was destroyed within seconds. Surprisingly, only 35 of the 97 people on board died in the incident as well as one fatality on the ground. The exact cause of the explosion still remains a mystery although sabotage seems to be a common theory. It is often said that if the Hindenburg had been filled with helium rather than hydrogen, the disaster would not have happened.

Procedure

1 Show your students the image and find out if they know anything about it.

2 Tell your students that you are going to read them a short text about the image. Tell them that they will probably hear some words that they don't recognize but that they should do their best not to let these impair overall comprehension.

3 Read out the text to your students. Speak clearly and at a relaxed pace.

4 Ask your students to relay back to you all the facts that they understood from the reading and write these in note form on the blackboard. Also, make a list of any new or problematic vocabulary/collocations/structures that were identified.

5 Read the text two more times. After each reading, try and elicit more facts and language from your students to add to the existing list on the board.

6 After the three readings, the board might look something like this:

Example *6 May, 1937*
36 people
sabotage
burst into flames
a masterpiece
helium rather than hydrogen
engineering
hold a record
the largest aircraft ever built
although
Lakehurst Naval Air Station, New Jersey
disaster struck
first transatlantic passenger flight of the year

Put your students into pairs or small groups and ask them to work together to reconstruct the text as accurately as they remember it. Tell them that they have to incorporate all of the facts and language items that have been written on the board.

7 Allow different groups to merge and compare their texts. During this step, every student has the right to make changes to his or her version—even if this means copying parts of another group's version.

8 Allow students to compare their texts with the original version.

9 If any additional questions arise (for example, why was the Hindenburg filled with hydrogen rather than helium?), ask your students to investigate these themselves as a homework task.

Variation

There are many different ways of carrying out a dictogloss. Some teachers feel that it is important for learners to make their own notes during the reading/listening process and then share these with their group members just prior to the text reconstruction step. Other teachers like to have a member from each group write up their final text on the board so that they can be compared and discussed. Overhead projectors are also suitable for this purpose.

2
Reading

For children learning to read, pictures are important for communicating the meaning contained within words. Why should it be any different when learning a foreign language? In the first activity of this chapter, we see how a single mental image, which is central to a text, may be exploited to support learners' reading comprehension. Subsequent activities make use of a commonly cited theory about a famous piece of western art, a sinister diary entry, and the story behind a police booking photograph. Also included is a basic idea for using images to set homework assignments.

2.1 The baby gorilla joke

Level Elementary +

Time 40 minutes

Aims To use an image to engage students with a text before reading and reinforce their understanding of it.

Preparation

Copy Worksheet 2.1a and cut into individual strips.

Worksheet 2.1a ✂

A man finds a baby gorilla in the street and takes him to the police.

He asks a policeman, 'What should I do with this baby gorilla?'

The policeman tells him to go to the zoo.

A week later the policeman sees the same man and the baby gorilla in the street.

'Didn't I tell you to take this baby gorilla to the zoo?' asks the policeman.

The man replies, 'I did take him to the zoo and today I'm taking him to the cinema.'

Photocopiable © Oxford University Press

Procedure

1 Read out the instructions below to your students clearly and slowly. Stop at any words they might not understand and explain them (using gesture, for example). Repeat the instructions and then ask students to relay them back to you before they start drawing. Help students with their drawings by showing them a picture of a baby gorilla.

I want you to draw a picture of a man and a baby gorilla standing in the street holding hands. The baby gorilla is eating an ice cream and the man is talking to a police officer. The police officer doesn't look happy. Draw two speech bubbles—one coming out of the man's mouth and another coming out of the police officer's mouth.

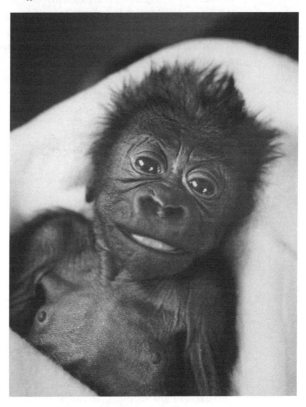

2 When your students have finished their drawings put them into pairs and ask them to consider what the man and the police officer are talking about. Ask them to write out a short dialogue.

3 While your students are writing, stick the six lines from the joke randomly on the walls around the classroom.

4 Ask for volunteer pairs to act out their dialogues for the rest of the class.

5 Tell students that you have a story for them and show them the pieces of text on the classroom walls. Ask students to go around the classroom, read all of the joke lines, and copy them into their notebooks in the correct order.

6 Allow students to check their results with each other before inviting individuals to recite the joke.

Variation

Instead of putting the joke lines on the wall, give out a different line to each student and, as a communicative exercise, ask them to work out the order of the joke without showing each other their lines.

Follow-up 1

To reactivate the language in the joke at later dates, ask your students to complete Worksheet 2.1b

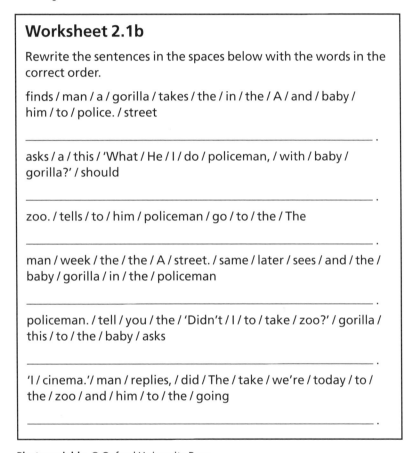

Worksheet 2.1b

Rewrite the sentences in the spaces below with the words in the correct order.

finds / man / a / gorilla / takes / the / in / the / A / and / baby / him / to / police. / street

_____ .

asks / a / this / 'What / He / I / do / policeman, / with / baby / gorilla?' / should

_____ .

zoo. / tells / to / him / policeman / go / to / the / The

_____ .

man / week / the / the / A / street. / same / later / sees / and / the / baby / gorilla / in / the / policeman

_____ .

policeman. / tell / you / the / 'Didn't / I / to / take / zoo?' / gorilla / this / to / the / baby / asks

_____ .

'I / cinema.'/ man / replies, / did / The / take / we're / today / to / the / zoo / and / him / to / the / going

_____ .

Photocopiable © Oxford University Press

Follow-up 2

Put the joke up on the classroom wall in large easy-to-read text. Make photocopies of your students' sketches from their notebooks and place these beside it. The images will constantly remind learners of the meaning of the language in the text which contains many areas of grammar that you will be able to refer to as and when necessary (the third person singular *s*, patterns of definite/indefinite article use, question forms, the use of the present continuous for future arrangements, etc.).

2.2 The story behind a piece of art

Level   Pre-Intermediate +

Time   90 minutes

Aims   To read about the story behind a piece of art. To practise structures containing prepositional phrases.

Preparation

Reading activities can be created using pictures of art and the texts that accompany them. Good resources of material include online galleries and encyclopaedias as well as art books and calendars (see Appendix 8c, page 134). Here we look at one of the most analysed works in Western art—Velázquez's *Las Meninas*. For this activity you will need a copy of Worksheet 2.2 for each student.

Procedure

1 Show your students *Las Meninas* and find out if they know anything about it.

2 Write the following questions on the board and ask students to copy them down before discussing them.

How many people are there in the painting?
Who do you think they are and when do you think they lived?
What do you think they are looking at?
Can you see the painter? What do you think he is painting?

Worksheet 2.2

Diego Velázquez (A), the Spanish Court Painter, is at work. He stands in front of a large canvas on the far left hand side of the picture, brushes in one hand and a palette in the other.

Five-year-old Margarita-Teresa (B), the King's daughter, stands in the centre of the painting between her two maids of honour (*meninas*). One of them, Doña María (C), offers the Princess a drink but she doesn't seem interested: There is clearly someone or something more interesting in the room.

The woman behind Doña Isabel (D), the maid of honour on the right, is the Princess's chaperone (E). She is talking to a bodyguard (F). Then in the background, standing in the doorway is Don José Nieto Velázquez (G). He may be a relative of the painter.

Two dwarfs on the right hand side of the picture complete Margarita-Teresa's entourage. Like the Princess and the painter, Maribarbola (H) is looking our way. Nicolasito (I) on the other hand is more interested in playing with the big sleepy dog (J) in the foreground.

So what is happening here? What is Diego Velázquez painting and what is his composition all about? As we look at the figures in his picture, why do many of them look back at us and make us feel as if we are the centre of attention? There is an important clue in the room. Above the head of the Princess, hanging on the back wall, there is something that looks like another painting. In fact, it is a mirror. What we are looking at is the reflection of Margarita-Teresa's parents.

The viewer is occupying the same space as King Felipe IV (K) and his Queen (L) who are posing to have their portraits painted. Perhaps their daughter and her entourage were brought into the room to relieve the boredom. Perhaps the King or Queen remarked that the scene in front of their eyes would make a good picture. Perhaps 200 years before the invention of photographic film and at the request of his employers, Velázquez has captured a real moment in time behind the scenes at the Royal Court.

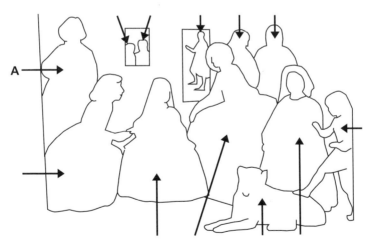

Photocopiable © Oxford University Press

3 Tell students that you have a text for them that should answer these questions. Give out copies of Worksheet 2.2, ask students to read the text and identify the people in the picture by labelling the diagram at the bottom of the page.

4 Let students compare their answers before conducting feedback.

Solution:

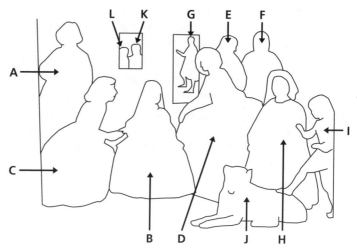

Follow-up

Ask your students to put their texts away and dictate the following paraphrased excerpts, each of which contains a prepositional phrase.

Diego Velázquez stands **in front of** *a large canvas* **on the far left hand side** *of the picture.*
Margarita-Teresa stands **in the centre of** *the painting* **between** *her two maids of honour.*
The woman **behind** *Doña Isabel is the Princess's chaperone.*
In the background, *standing* **in the doorway** *is Don José Nieto Velázquez.*
There is a sleepy dog **in the foreground.**
Above *the head of the Princess, hanging* **on the back wall,** *there is something that looks like another painting.*
Perhaps the King or Queen remarked that the scene **in front of** *their eyes would make a good picture.*
Velázquez has captured a real moment in time **behind** *the scenes at the Royal Court.*

Let students refer back to the text to check what they have written. Following this, ask them to translate the dictated sentences into their own language on a separate piece of paper. Finally, ask them to translate the sentences from their own language back into English (they should do this without looking at either the original text or at the dictated sentences).

Comments

1 In 1957 Pablo Picasso painted a number of interpretations of *Las Meninas*. These can be found online and shown to your students alongside the original to practise the language of comparison.

2 Virtually any piece of art that has been written about can be used for similar reading activities. Other good examples include Picasso's *Guernica* and Théodore Géricault's *The Raft of the Medusa*.

2.3 Illustrating a text

Level Intermediate +

Time 40 minutes

Aims To personalize a text by illustrating it. To distinguish between past simple and past continuous structures.

Preparation

1 Make a copy of Worksheet 2.3 for each student and cut it in half along the scissor line.

2 Supply your students with colour pencils.

Worksheet 2.3a

'I was walking along a path with two friends. The sun was setting. Suddenly the sky turned blood red. I paused, feeling exhausted, and leaned on the fence – there was blood and tongues of fire above the blue-black fjord and the city. My friends walked on, and I stood there trembling with anxiety – and I sensed an infinite scream passing through nature.'

Worksheet 2.3b

Look at Munch's 1892 diary entry again. Look at the parts in **bold**. In each case, can you remember which form (past simple or past continuous) the verbs were in?

'I **walked / was walking** along a path with two friends. The sun **set / was setting** Suddenly the sky **turned / was turning** blood red. I **paused / was pausing**, feeling exhausted, and **leaned / was leaning** on the fence – there was blood and tongues of fire above the blue-black fjord and the city. My friends **walked / were walking** on, and I **stood / was standing** there trembling with anxiety – and I **sensed / was sensing** an infinite scream passing through nature.'

Photocopiable © Oxford University Press

Procedure

1 Give out copies of the full text (Worksheet 2.3a). Invite students to read it aloud and ask them if they can guess where it came from (poem, film, novel, etc). Explain any unknown words.

2 Tell your students that you will tell them where the text came from but first you would like them to illustrate it. Give out paper and colour pencils.

3 Allow your students to share and compare their artwork.

4 Tell your students that the text comes from a 1892 diary entry from a Norwegian artist called Edvard Munch. Ask them what kind of man they think he was.

5 Take back the texts from your students and give out copies of Worksheet 2.3b to be completed.

6 Let your students compare their answers before allowing them to look back at the original text.

Variation 1

The diary entry describes a recurring vision that was said to haunt Munch. It is the source of inspiration for his most famous painting, *Scream*, which can easily be found online, in art books, calendars, etc. Following step 4, show this piece of artwork to your learners and let them compare what they have drawn with Munch's masterpiece.

Variation 2

Choose a song with good imagery or descriptive elements, give out copies of the lyrics and ask your students to illustrate them. This works well if you can lead your students to think they are illustrating poems rather than songs. It means that the listening stage will come as a pleasant surprise. Some good songs to use include, *Good Year for the Roses*, *She's Leaving Home*, and *Space Oddity*.

2.4 Image quests

Level Intermediate +

Time This activity should proceed over three stages:
STAGE 1 Teacher sets task (20 minutes)
STAGE 2 Students plan a talk in class or at home (deadline to be set by teacher)
STAGE 3 Students give talks (time dependent on number of students)

Aims To research the facts, events, people, and issues behind a historic news image. To present this to the rest of the class.

Preparation

Find a selection of historic news images to take into class (see Appendix 8e, page 134). Examples could include The Hindenburg Disaster (Activity 1.5), Buzz Aldrin on the Moon (above), or historic police booking photographs (Activity 2.5).

Procedure

1 One by one, show the images to your students and find out how much they know about each one.

2 Tell students that you would like each of them to choose a different image—ideally the one that interests them the most. Tell them that they are going to find out about the stories behind their images and then give short talks to present their research to the rest of the class. Write a list of possible points for consideration on the board.

Example   *What happened?*
Where did it happen?
When did it happen?
Who was involved (people, organizations, countries, etc.)?
How and why did it happen?
Background events?
Outcomes?
Issues?
Opinion?

3 Discuss potential sources on the Internet that will be helpful to your students as they research their images (online encyclopaedias, etc.). If students have Internet access during class time, allow them to find and print off three or four texts that relate to their images. If not, they will have to find these at home.

4 Encourage students to look at their texts critically—some texts will be more authoritative than others and there will often be factual discrepancies between them.

5 Ask your students to read their texts, identify the main points, and plan their talks. Make it clear that you do not want students to read directly from their downloaded texts although they can make and use cue cards if they like.

6 Students will also have to consider how they are going to display their images during their talks. They could be encouraged to prepare computer presentations or slide shows (see Appendix 3, page 131) containing their image and any others that are relevant to it.

7 When your students come to give their talks, encourage participant interaction by asking everyone else to think of a question that can be asked at the end.

Variation 1

Rather than giving talks on the stories behind images, ask your students to create visually stimulating, informative posters for the classroom wall.

Variation 2

Instead of historic photographs, ask students to investigate the stories behind famous pieces of art. Alternatively, use well-known self-portraits to encourage them to find out about the artists behind them.

2.5 The story behind an image

Level Upper-intermediate +

Time 60 minutes

Aims To read about the story behind a newsworthy image. To practise passive structures.

Preparation

Make photocopies of Worksheet 2.5 for each student.

Procedure

1 Show your students the police booking photograph (or 'mug shot') of Patty Hearst and ask the questions below. If any of your students recognize the image and know the story of Patty Hearst, ask them if they could keep quiet at this stage.

How old do you think this woman looks?
What sort of background do you think she comes from?
What do you think she was arrested for?

2   Give out copies of Worksheet 2.5 and ask your learners to read the text and find out why her case was unusual. Encourage them to work out the meaning of any unknown words or language whenever it is possible. Offer help whenever it is not.

3   Show your learners that there is a glossary to be completed at the bottom of the text and ask them to fill in the blanks using the words and phrases in **bold**.

4   Allow your learners to compare their answers with each other before conducting class feedback.

Answers:

claimed responsibility for	admitted to
made a clean getaway	escaped from the crime scene
gripped	fascinated
denounced	harshly criticized/disowned
making the headlines	in the news
wounded two bystanders	injured 2 innocent people
high-profile	important; well-publicized
culminated	reached the highest point
video footage	recorded film
commuted	reduced
twist in the plot	surprise in the story
brainwashed	mind-altered through extreme mental pressure.

5   Ask your students to put their texts away and dictate the following seven sentences about Patty Hearst.

She told police that she had been kept in closets and abused both physically and mentally.
She was arrested in a San Francisco apartment with other SLA members.
She was caught on camera taking part in a bank robbery.
She was granted a full pardon by Bill Clinton
She was kidnapped by an urban terrorist group known as the SLA.
She was released from prison after serving 22 months of her sentence.
She was sentenced to 7 years in prison.

6   Ask your students to put the sentences into the correct chronological order.

7   Allow your students to compare their answers before giving feedback.

Variation 1

Following her arrest, a more sinister-looking picture of Patty Hearst appeared on the cover of *Time* magazine (see below). Try introducing the above activity using the two different versions of the mug shot. Divide your students into two groups and show the original mug shot to group A and the *Time* magazine cover to group B. Ask the same questions as in step 1 and compare the answers that your students give. Perhaps the results of this 'experiment' will demonstrate that images in the media can influence public opinion.

Worksheet 2.5
Patty Hearst

At 9:40 am on April 15, 1974, four women and a man walked into a San Francisco bank, stole $10,000, **wounded two bystanders**, and **made a clean getaway** in a waiting car. Those behind the crime belonged to an urban terrorist group known as the Symbionese Liberation Army.

The SLA had already been **making the headlines**. Just 10 weeks before, they had **claimed responsibility for** the **high-profile** abduction of a 19-year old girl called Patricia Hearst, the granddaughter of William Randolph Hearst, a legendary newspaper publisher.

The story **gripped** America and the public followed the events and formed opinions as a series of recorded messages from the SLA heard Hearst grow increasingly sympathetic towards her captors, and critical of her parents' efforts to meet their demands. This seemed to **culminate** two months after the kidnapping when she **denounced** her family and announced that she had joined the group.

But even the police examining **video footage** of the bank robbery could not have expected this latest **twist in the plot**: Among the 5 robbers caught on camera that Monday morning in April was Patricia Hearst herself, armed, elegant, and shouting commands at customers.

On September 18 the next year, she was arrested in a San Francisco apartment with other SLA members. Following her capture, her revolutionary attitude soon changed to that of **brainwashed** victim. She spoke of how her captors had kept her in closets and abused her both physically and mentally.

Hearst was charged with bank robbery and in 1976, following a controversial trial, she was sentenced to 7 years in prison. She served only 22 months of her term which was **commuted** by President Jimmy Carter and in 2001, Patricia Hearst was granted a full pardon by President Bill Clinton.

Glossary

_____	admitted to
_____	escaped from the crime scene
_____	fascinated
_____	harshly criticized/disowned
_____	important; well-publicized
_____	in the news
_____	injured two innocent people
_____	reached the highest point
_____	recorded film
_____	reduced
_____	surprise in the story
_____	mind-altered through extreme mental pressure.

Photocopiable © Oxford University Press

Patricia Hearst, alias Tania

Variation 2

The full fascinating story of Patty Hearst can easily be found online. It can be visually supported and used for an engaging storytelling activity in the classroom. Other images that are central to the story include:

- a photo of Patty and fiancé Steven Weed before the abduction
- a film poster of *Citizen Kane* (the film is said to portray the life of William Randolph Hearst, Patty's grandfather)
- a publicity image released by the SLA in which Patty poses in combat gear
- original footage of the bank robbery (can be found on video-sharing sites)
- original CBS News reports (can be found on video-sharing sites)
- the trailer for a 2004 film about Patty Hearst directed by Robert Stone (can be found on video-sharing sites)
- FBI Wanted posters for Patty and the other SLA members.

Follow-up 1

For homework, ask your students to find out more about the Patty Hearst story. (What were the demands of the SLA following her abduction? What happened between the bank robbery and Hearst's arrest? Why was her trial controversial? etc.)

Follow-up 2

Ask students to tell each other or write about notorious crime stories from their own countries. Perhaps they can complement these by finding any relevant images (mug shots, etc.) online.

Follow-up 3

Refer back to the Patty Hearst mug shot whenever you want to revise the passive structures that were looked at there.

3
Writing

An elephant in the fridge; a pig in boots; a woman standing on a ledge battling with the police; what is going on? Many of the images in this chapter cry out to be explained. Others ask for their visual messages to be put into words or complemented with captions. All of them aim to motivate and encourage language learners to write.

3.1 Photographic memories

Level Beginner +

Time 15 minutes per image

Aims To write a description of an image from memory.

Preparation

For this activity, you will need a stimulating picture—one in which there is a lot happening. The images in Activities 1.1, 2.5, or 3.2 would work well.

Procedure

1 Ask your students if they believe that some people can really have photographic memories. Ask them if they know anyone who claims to do so.

2 Tell students that you are going to do an experiment to find out who has the best photographic memory in the class. Tell them that they are going to see an image for exactly one minute and after that they will have to write down absolutely everything they remember about it.

3 Show students the image for one minute.

4 Ask students to write a description of the image from memory in as much detail as they can. Allow access to bilingual dictionaries if possible/necessary.

5 Everyone should read out their texts and decide who has the most photographic memory in the class. Finally, collect in the texts for correction.

Comment

This activity could be used as a follow-up to any of those in the previous two chapters which aim to equip students with the language of image descriptions (see Activities 1.1, 1.4, 2.2, or 2.5, for example).

3.2 Why is there an elephant in the fridge?

Level Elementary +

Time 30 minutes

Aims To write an explanation for an unlikely situation.

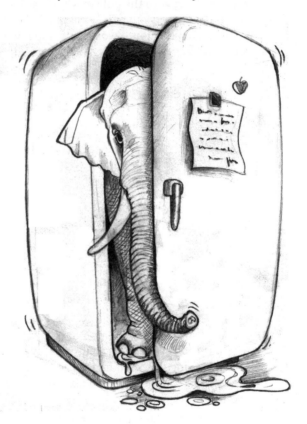

Preparation

Make copies of Worksheet 3.2 for your students.

Procedure

1 Ask your students to close their eyes and talk them through the following imaginary situation. While you are doing so, stop and ask questions whenever appropriate in order to keep students involved and make the scenario more real.

You are on your own at home. Perhaps you are in your bedroom reading a book or watching television in the living room.

Ask individuals which room they are in and what they are doing:

You hear the front door open and someone walks in—someone that you live with such as a flatmate, your son, your mother, etc.

Ask individuals who the person is:

You see/hear the person walk into the kitchen, put something down on the table—probably bags of shopping—walk over to the fridge, open it, and scream.

2 Ask students to suggest possible reasons for the scream before showing them the image opposite.

3 Tell your students the following:

Oh dear! Obviously the person who got a fright didn't see the note that you left attached to the fridge door with a magnet.

4 Give out copies of Worksheet 3.2. Students complete the note and explain exactly why there is an elephant in the fridge.

Worksheet 3.2

Dear _____

If you open the fridge, be prepared for a surprise. There is an elephant inside. There is a perfectly good explanation for this …

_____

_____

_____

_____

_____

_____

_____

_____

_____

_____

_____

_____

_____

_____

_____

_____

_____

Photocopiable © Oxford University Press

3.3 Thought bubbles

Level Elementary +

Time 20–30 minutes

Aims To imagine and write what animals think about. To practise verbs like *wish* and *wonder*.

Preparation

1 Choose a few pictures in which animals are looking pensive or seem to be communicating. The larger the variety of animals—both wild and domesticated—the better.

2 Make photocopies of the thought bubbles on the next page (photocopy one page for every student in the class).

Procedure

1 Stick one of the images on the board and draw a large thought bubble coming from the animal's head (see picture above). Elicit some of the things that different animals think about and write these on the board in note form.

2 Ask your students to suggest things that could be written in the thought bubble and add these to the board.

3 Write a few pieces of language on the board that could help your students' imaginations.

Example *I wish I could …*
I wish I was …
I wonder …

4 Give out the photocopied thought bubbles to your students (one sheet per person) and ask them to cut or tear out the individual bubbles. Meanwhile, you can put the other pictures up around the classroom walls.

Photocopiable © Oxford University Press

5 Ask students to go around the gallery, write in their thought bubbles, and attach them to the animals in the pictures (using glue, sticky tape, etc.). Allow access to bilingual dictionaries if possible. Make sure they realize that a picture can have more than one thought bubble placed beside it.

6 Once this has been done, identify who wrote what and offer corrections.

Variation 1

This activity could be given a competitive edge similar to that in a caption competition. If you have a class blog or image-sharing page (see Appendix 2, page 130), upload a picture like the one at the beginning of this activity and invite your students to leave comments, notes or captions. Have a vote to decide who the winner is.

Variation 2

Try using a combination of speech and thought bubbles with any of the following:

- famous paintings (*Mona Lisa*, *Las Meninas*, Klimt's *The Kiss*, Munch's *Scream*, etc.)
- other pictures in this book (images from Activities 1.1, 2.4, 3.2, for example)
- adverts from magazines.
- photographs of statues and sculptures from around your town (see image from Activity 4.1).

Variation 3

Cut a comic strip out of a newspaper and use correction fluid to hide the words in the speech bubbles (leave the bubble outlines intact). Make enlarged photocopies of the blank cartoon strips, give them out to your students, and have them improvise the story by filling in the speech bubbles. Later, allow students to compare their work with each other's and then the original.

3.4 Advert defacement therapy

Level Elementary +

Time 30 minutes

Aims To look at adverts and write captions or paragraphs that describe what the creators are saying to the public.

Preparation

1 Find about ten adverts from various magazines or newspapers that claim in an indirect yet blatant way that a product will do one of the following:
- make your life fantastic and glamorous
- make you happier
- improve your social life
- make you look younger and more beautiful
- make you more sexually attractive
- make you just like the celebrity or model in the advert.

2 Put these adverts up around the classroom walls and number them with sticky labels.

Procedure

1 As students enter the room, invite them to walk around and look at the adverts on the walls.

2 Once everyone has arrived, tell your students that you want them to go around the gallery and put into words exactly what the advert says to the viewer. Give them an example.

Example *These cereal bars are so low in calories that the more you eat, the thinner you will become. As a result you will be beautiful and happy. Don't forget to eat a whole box every day or you will turn into a fatty.*

3 Ask students to go around the gallery (as individuals or pairs) and write similar captions for each advert. These should be written in notebooks or on a single sheet of paper so that they can be handed in to you for correction at the end of the day. Make sure students write the advert numbers beside their captions.

4 Once everyone has finished this task, gather everyone around in a circle. Have individuals read out their ideas while the rest of the class guesses which advert is being referred to and helps with language correction.

Variation 1

Tell your students about 'the Bubble Project' (see Comment below). For step 3, have them make speech bubbles which they then stick on to the adverts on the walls.

Variation 2

One excellent way of gaining insight into the minds of advertisers and the tricks and techniques that they employ is to compare a number of adverts for similar products (perfume, cars, watches, etc.). Turn your classroom into a themed advert gallery.

A good way to do this would be to obtain a women's magazine and a men's magazine and cut out all the adverts for perfume, for example, number them, and stick them on the classroom walls. Invite your students to browse the gallery and ask them to decide exactly who or what type of person each advert is aimed at. They should then write a brief outline of how they came to their conclusion. In doing so, they may want to describe factors such as colour, shapes and lines, objects, people, animals, places, actions, emotion, symbolism, font, and slogans, etc.

Follow-up

Correct your students' work and give it back to them. Relocate the adverts to a single wall in the classroom (to economize on space) and stick up a selection of your students' captions beside them.

Comment

This idea was inspired by 'the Bubble Project', a counter-attack on the influx of advertising messages in public spaces. Frustrated advertiser Ji Lee attached thousands of sticky white blank speech bubbles on posters all over New York City and almost immediately people started to fill them in.

3.5 Naughty pet wanted poster

Level   Elementary +

Time   This activity should proceed over two days
   DAY 1   Students write anecdotes about naughty pets: 40 minutes
   DAY 2   Students use their corrected texts to make 'Wanted' posters:
   30 minutes

Aims   To write a narrative text about naughty things that pets have done.

Preparation

In preparation for this activity, ask your students to bring in
photographs of any pets they have.

Procedure

1   Show your students the above picture and make sure they know
   what the word 'naughty' means.

2   Ask students to guess why the dog looks so guilty. What has she
   done? Write ideas and any new or relevant language on the board as
   it arises.

3   Ask students to take out the photographs of their pets and introduce
   them to the rest of the class. Find out if anyone has a pet that has
   ever done something naughty and share stories. You can also ask
   students to think about incidents involving pets they have had, or
   pets belonging to neighbours, friends, or family members, etc.

4   Tell students that you would like everyone to write out a short
   anecdote about a naughty pet. If they don't have an anecdote, they
   can invent one about the dog in the picture.

5   Encourage students to prepare their texts by

   • writing out the main points of the anecdote in chronological order
   • listing all the verbs that they are going to use

- deciding what past tense (simple, continuous, or perfect) they are going to use the verbs in.

6 Collect in all the texts for marking.

7 The next day, give back all corrected texts and ask students to make 'Wanted' posters for their pets. Ask them to include the following:
- the naughty pet's name
- a sketch of the pet (a photocopy of a photograph would be even better)
- the 'crime' (this will be the students' re-written texts)
- the reward for capture.

Variation 1

This activity works best if you can supply students with a model text and 'Wanted' poster before they create their own. Write out a short anecdote about a cat or dog in your life. Stick a photograph of the pet on the board and label it in the same way as the picture of the naughty dog above. Introduce it and ask your students to guess what naughty thing it did.

Variation 2

The same activity could be done for naughty brothers and sisters.

3.6 Journalists

Level Elementary +

Time 45 minutes

Aims To report the story behind a picture in a short newspaper article.

Preparation

1 For this activity, you will need a newspaper or magazine article which revolves around an accompanying picture or series of pictures. For example, the image on page 48 tells the story of the theft of the paintings, Munch's *Scream* and *Madonna*, from the Munch Museum, Oslo, on the morning of Sunday 22 August 2004. The paintings were recovered two years later, damp and slightly damaged. The photograph appeared in newspapers around the world.

2 Once you have selected a good picture or series of pictures, familiarize yourself with the main points in the text. Since your students are going to interview you about these, you may wish to make notes.

Procedure

1 Show your students the image(s) and ask them to hypothesize about the content of the accompanying story. For some images this might be quite difficult and you may have to give clues or ask questions to help.

Example *What do you think these men are carrying?*
The building in the background is a famous museum in Oslo, Norway.
Do you think the men work for the museum?

2 Tell students that they are journalists and that they are going to write a short article to accompany the image. Before doing so, they have to interview you (the teacher) to find out the facts.

3 Allow your students to ask you as many questions as they like about the news story. Encourage them to make notes while they do so. Invent any extra information you wish.

4 Ask your students to use the notes they made to plan their newspaper reports. Ask them to decide what they are going to include in their texts and what they are going to omit.

5 While your students write their newspaper reports, be on hand to clarify facts and help with language.

6 Finally, put the original text up on the wall and allow your students to compare it with their own versions.

Variation

Instead of a newspaper story, students could prepare television news reports or radio newsflashes. These could be filmed or recorded in class.

3.7 The back of the box

Level Pre-intermediate +

Time 60 minutes

Aims To write an imaginary synopsis for a film. To prepare for this by brainstorming and arranging ideas.

Preparation

For this activity, you will need a few film images—preferably ones that your students will not have seen (see image below). Possible sources of film images include empty DVD or video boxes, downloaded film images, trailers on video-sharing sites, etc. (see Appendix 8c, page 134 for more ideas).

CRAWLING, SLIMY THINGS
TERROR-BENT ON
DESTROYING THE WORLD!

the
Brain
Eaters

EDWIN NELSON · JOANNA LEE · ALAN FROST · Produced by EDWIN NELSON · Directed by BRUNO VESOTA · Story & Screenplay by GORDON URQUHART-AN AMERICAN INTERNATIONAL PICTURE

Procedure

1 Write *You can't judge a book by its cover* on the board and ask your students if they can guess what this well-known English saying means (i.e. *We should not base our opinions of people and things on the way they look*). Ask your students whether or not they agree with the idea.

2 Tell students that they are going to take part in an experiment. Tell them that they are going to determine whether or not it is possible to judge a film by its poster/trailer. Show your students the film images one by one and in each case, ask questions.

Example *Has anyone seen this film? If so, tell the rest of the class about it.*
When do you think it was made?
What type of film do you think it is? (horror, science fiction, romantic comedy, children's, etc.)
When do you think it is set (i.e. when does the story take place?)
Where do you think it is set? (i.e. where does the story take place?)
Who do you think it is aimed at? (i.e. target audience)
What do you think it is about?
Does it look good or bad? Would you like to see it?

3 Ask your students to make their own conclusions about the experiment. Remind them that film posters are adverts and ask what sort of information the creators want to communicate to us.

4 Show your students the images again and, this time, ask them to decide which film looks the most predictable. Make sure students know that if a film is predictable, it is obvious what is going to happen in it. Have a vote to decide which is the most predictable film.

5 Tell your students to imagine that they have changed their jobs: They now write summaries of films for the back of the DVD boxes. Tell them that their task today is to write a summary for the film that was chosen as the most predictable. Tell them they will have to be imaginative and invent the details. Ask questions and brainstorm students for ideas and write these up on the blackboard.

Example *What do the Brain Eaters look like?*
Where are they from?
What happens to people when they get their brains eaten?
What happens to the Brain Eaters in the end of the film?

6 Ask your students to arrange their ideas into the order that they are going to write about them. Ask students what tense they will be writing in (mostly present simple) and then ask them to write their summaries. Set a minimum length for the summary (150 words would be suitable). Provide linguistic support as required. You may also decide to supply bilingual dictionaries.

7 Allow students to read out their summaries or put them on the walls for everyone to read before taking them in for marking.

Variation 1

On many cinematic or encyclopaedic websites, the entry for any film offers a brief synopsis of it. Print these off and use them in conjunction with the images for any of the following reading activities.

- Let students compare the summaries they wrote with the real ones.
- Give students the synopsis and ask them to design the film poster (see Activity 2.2).
- Create a gallery of film posters in the classroom. Make copies of all the synopses on a worksheet and ask your students to go around the gallery and match the films with their synopses.
- Use with reading activities in which the image serves to engage students with the text (see Activities 2.2 and 2.5, for example).

Variation 2

Step 2 involves the teacher repeatedly asking some good film questions. After hearing them a number of times, ask your students if they can recall them.

Variation 3

Rather than asking students to write summaries, ask them to write imaginary pieces of dialogue.

3.8 Incident report

Level Intermediate +

Time 30 minutes

Aims To invent and write about the details of an incident.

Preparation

Find a photograph of a newsworthy incident. This activity uses as an example a photograph from the 1940s.

Procedure

1 Show your students the photograph and use it elicit/teach vocabulary or language that is central to it.

Example *a ledge above a doorway*
the police
a safety net (has been put up)
a crowd (of onlookers)

2 Ask your students questions about the scene and write additional language on the board as it arises.

Example *Where and when do you think this incident took place?*
What do you think is happening?
How do you think it started?
How did it end?
Do you think the police are trying to help the woman or arrest her?
Why is the woman fighting with the police?
Is she suicidal? If so why?

3 Give your students the following task (this can be dictated to them or written on the board).

> You are a policeman/policewoman who was involved in the incident in the picture. Write a report explaining what happened. How did it start? How did you and your colleagues get involved? How did you deal with it? How did the incident end?

4 Encourage your students to plan their reports using any key words or language that were written on the board during steps 1 and 2. Also ask them to consider what tenses and structures they are most likely to use (past simple, past continuous, there was/were).

5 Allow students to write their reports.

Comment

Edna Egbert, the woman in the photograph, was reportedly upset because her soldier son had not been in touch for a year. In the picture, which was taken on 19 March 1942, she is seen battling with police as they try to prevent her from jumping off a window ledge at her home in Brooklyn. They managed to distract her until a safety net had been put up below, then pushed her into it after which the crowd of 600 onlookers dispersed.

3.9 Story building

Level Intermediate +

Time 30 minutes

Aims To work in a group to create a story.

Preparation

Find a picture that lends itself to telling a story.

Procedure

1 Show your students the picture and ask questions that will engage them with the characters in it.

Example *Where and when do you think this photograph was taken?*
What time do you think it was taken?
How long do you think the couple on the left have known each other?
Do you think the waiter is happy in his job? Why/why not?
Do you think he is married, single or divorced?
Do you think there is anything in his life that he would like to change? What?

2 Arrange students into groups of three or four and ask each group to sit in a circle. Tell groups that they are each going to improvise a story about the waiter in the picture and ask them to give him a name.

3 Write a few possible story opening lines on the board. You can also elicit ideas from students.

Example *(Waiter's name) was lonely and needed to find love.*
One night, as he was closing the café, (waiter's name) made a decision that would change his life forever.
It had been a long day and (waiter's name) really wanted to go home.

4 Once each group has decided how their story is going to begin, members should take it in turn to add to it. Turns should proceed clockwise from the first storyteller.

5 Once a group has completed their story, ask all members to work together to write it down. During the writing process, group members can make as many changes or improvements to their stories as they like.

6 Invite a storyteller from each group to share their story with the rest of the class.

Variation 1

Sometimes circle storytelling works best if group members have to complete their story in a specific number of turns (twelve, for example). This can prevent stories from getting too long and losing direction.

Variation 2

Show students two unrelated images (the ones on the previous two pages for example) and ask them to write a story that connects them in some way or another.

3.10 Using titles

Level Intermediate +

Time 45 minutes

Aims To write titles for pieces of art. To consider how a title can be essential to appreciating a piece of art.

Preparation

1 Prepare a gallery or slide show (see Appendix 3, page 131) of pieces of art with good titles (see Appendix 8d, page 134). Look out for any of the following:

- titles which contain interesting grammar or language
- titles which are vital for understanding (at least partly) the work as a whole
- titles which cause the viewer to see the work in a way that it would not otherwise be seen.

The upside down tree people pray to their spiky gods (Jo Wray)

Example
- John Baldessari: *Throwing four balls in the air to get a square (best of thirty-six tries)*
- Damien Hirst: *The physical impossibility of death in the mind of someone living*
- Yeames: *And when did you last see your father?*
- Salvador Dalí: *Dream caused by the flight of a bee around a pomegranate a second before awakening* (surrealists in general may work well for this activity)
- Donna Ferrato: *Lisa—moments after her husband beat her*
- Any piece from Philip-Lorca DiCorcia's Hollywood series. For example: *Eddie Anderson; 21 Years Old; Houston, Texas; 20 dollars* (The titles in this series tell us exactly how much the photographer paid the models to persuade them to sign a release form.)

- Any piece from Bill Owen's Suburbia series. For example:
  I wanted Christina to learn some responsibility for cleaning her room but it didn't work (The photographs in this series are accompanied by statements from the subjects involved in them.)
- A piece of untitled work (Gregory Crewdson's photographs are thought-provoking and usually untitled.)
- Picasso's 1901 self portrait *Yo Picasso* (Students may not realize that this is a picture of Picasso until they are given the title.)
- Any still life (a good contextualized example of the adjective 'still')

2 Number the pieces on display so that they can be referred to.

3 Prepare a sheet which contains the titles that you will be displaying with the names of the artists beside each one. Make copies of this sheet for your students. Part of this activity will involve students matching these titles with the pieces of art. It is important, therefore, that you list the titles randomly.

Procedure

1 Show your students the slide show or let them browse the gallery of the selected work.

2 Discuss the pieces one by one with your class. Find out if your learners have seen them before, what they think of them, etc.

3 Tell your students to look at the artwork a second time. This time you want them to invent and write down a title for each one. They can do this in pairs or small groups if they like.

4 Let everyone compare and share their ideas. You could come to a class consensus or have a vote for the best title in each case.

5 Tell your students that you are going to give them a copy of all the real titles of the work on display (see Preparation, step 3). Tell them that their task is to match these with the pieces of artwork. Give a copy of the sheet to each student and ask them to carry out the task individually. If you are using a slide show, play it as a continuous loop, with each slide displayed for a few seconds.

6 Go over the pieces one at a time and find out how your students' attitudes towards them have changed now that they know the titles.

Variation 1

Give your students the list of titles before they see the artwork itself. Ask them to describe how they imagine the pieces to look before seeing them. Alternatively, refer students to an image search engine (see Appendix 1, page 129) to see the pieces of artwork for themselves. This can be a good opportunity for teaching students how to use online image search engines (see Activity 5.1).

Variation 2

Rather than giving your students a list of the titles, dictate them or use them as the basis for a running dictation (see Activity 1.2).

Variation 3

Use the format of this activity for any of the following:

- adverts from magazines and their slogans (cover up the slogans)
- cartoons and their captions
- films and their titles (films could be themes: *James Bond* films, films by Alfred Hitchcock, etc.).

Follow-up

For higher-level groups, ask each student to select two or three pieces of artwork from the activity and write a paragraph for each in which they state:

- their attitude to the piece of art and understanding of it before knowing the title
- how these changed after knowing the title.

4
Speaking

Can you imagine a friend showing you his or her holiday photographs in silence? Many of the speaking activities in this chapter centre around the personal connections that students make with images. Others exploit controversy, current affairs, or student curiosity to seed discussion. Finally, a number of activities make use of images of people. Humans are, after all, obsessed with other humans and the most convenient way of bringing a new person into the classroom is via a photograph.

4.1 Local corners

Level Beginner +

Time 30–45 minutes, depending on the number of pictures obtained.

Aims To describe the locations of local points of interest. To use images as a springboard for discussion.

Preparation

1 If you and your students are neighbours, living, working, or studying in the same town or city, obtain a good number of local photographs. Possible resources include local newspapers and magazines, directories, tourist guides, postcards, and the Internet. For a personal touch, a camera (or phone camera) is the best option. Look out for:

- interesting buildings
- public art (sculptures, murals, statues, graffiti, etc.)
- memorials and monuments
- museums, galleries, libraries, and theatres
- interesting graphics and designs (shop signs, etc.)
- notable bars, restaurants, shops, hotels, markets, etc.

2 Decide how you are going to display the images (print paper copies, computer slide show, etc.) and prepare the display.

Procedure

1 Show your students the photographs of your town and in each case elicit the exact location of each subject. Focus on prepositions and write them on the board as and when they arise.

Example *It's ...*
in/on (name of street/road, etc.)
on the corner of ...
at the bottom/top of ...
half way up ...
beside/behind/between ...
near/close to ...
on the left/right hand side of ...
in the middle of ...

Refer to a map of your town or use an online location finder (see Appendix 7a, page 133) for clarification as necessary.

2 In each case, use the photographs as springboards for discussion and continue to write new language on the board.

Example *What do you know about it?*
Have you ever been there and what is it like? (Tourist attractions, restaurants, galleries, etc.)
Would you recommend it to someone visiting your area? (Tourist attractions, restaurants, galleries, etc.)
Does it contribute negatively or positively to your environment? (Public art, buildings, graffiti, design, etc.)
Was it worth the money? (Public art, buildings, etc.)
When was it made/built/opened and what was there before? (Public art, buildings, shops, restaurants, monuments, etc.)

3 Once you have gone through the entire slide show, repeat it and use it to recall the contexts of all of the new language that has been written on the board. Work together as a whole class to recreate the examples which contain the new words or structures, drill them, and ask your students to write them down.

Example *Botero's cat is at the bottom of la Rambla del Raval on the right-hand side. It used to be in Plaça de Blanquema.*

Variation 1

Ask students to give directions to each location in the pictures from a given starting point (your school, for example).

Variation 2

This activity can be turned into a listening exercise. Before showing the photographs to your class, describe the locations yourself and ask your students to write down (i.e. not shout out) the local points of interest that they think you are referring to.

Variation 3

Try using old pictures of your town. This is good for eliciting *used to* (*This is where the old theatre used to be; this pub used to be a church*, etc.).

Comment

The format of this activity can be used for virtually any situation in which teachers and students find themselves in the same place at the same time. Teachers who have just arrived in a new place can exploit pictures of local points of interest to learn from their new students. Similarly, for groups that have recently gathered in a new town or city (on an intensive summer course, for example) a handful of pictures will allow students to share new knowledge and experience of their new environment.

4.2 Colour symbolism

Level Beginner +

Time 60 minutes

Aims To share and compare personal and cultural perceptions of different colours.

Preparation

Set up a computer with Internet access in the classroom (optional).

Procedure

1 Describe the following image to your students in as much detail as possible. Tell them exactly what is going on and who is involved but make no reference to any colours.

Example *This is a photograph of a Japanese wedding procession. The bride and groom are both wearing kimonos—the national Japanese costume. The bride is wearing a hat which covers most of her hair. They are in a boat, sailing through a garden after the wedding ceremony.*

2 Ask your learners what colours they expect to see in the picture (most importantly, black and white). After discussing the possibilities, show your class the image.

3 Find out about your students' own cultural colour associations with the following:

- funerals
- weddings
- baby boys (how they are dressed, for example)
- baby girls (as above).

4 Draw the following grid on the board and ask your students to copy it on to A4-sized sheets of paper.

Pink	Grey	Yellow	Brown	Orange	Purple
Blue	Red	Green	White		Black

5 If you have Internet access in the classroom, an image search engine (see Appendix 1, page 129) can be excellent for showing colours to language learners. For example, search for 'pink' and you might expect to see a pink rose, the Pink Panther, a pink dress, etc.

6 Tell your students that they are going to play a game. Put them into pairs or small groups. If you have a multicultural class, try to keep students from the same cultural background together.

7   Point out to students that, in English, it is quite common to describe a colour by placing a noun in front of it which functions as an adjective. Give some examples (pea green, blood red, etc.). Again, if possible, you could show students these examples using an image search engine.

8   Ask each pair or small group to think of eleven of their own word pairs—one for each colour. They should write these in their grids in the corresponding colour boxes. The first pair to complete the task wins.

9   Allow different pairs or groups to share their results. Write the best ones in the grid on the board.

10 Play another round of the game. This time you want students to think of an adjective or abstract noun for each colour on the grid. This will be an opportunity for students to compare their own cultural colour associations. You can start them off by giving a few examples of your own. Some typical western ideas might include: blue: royalty, red: danger, yellow: cowardice, green: envy, white: surrender, black: death.

11 Play one more round of the game. This time ask students to think of any product, brand, or company that they associate with each colour.

Variation

Image organizers (see Appendix 4, page 131) allow you to carry out simple image manipulations. Use such an application to convert colourful pictures into black and white. The activity outlined above could be introduced by showing students the black and white versions and asking them to predict the colour schemes before showing them the original, non-manipulated images. This activity could also be done using a standard television set: simply pause a film at a colourful moment and turn down the colour.

Follow-up

Steps 8 and 9 provide students with an excellent opportunity to build up an awareness of how collocations work. Create a worksheet like the one on page 62 that lists all the word pairs that your students thought of and add a few of your own. For homework, or in a computer room, ask students to type all of the word pairs into an Internet search engine and write down and compare their frequencies (i.e. the number of 'results' or 'hits' that are obtained in an Internet search). When using search engines in this way, phrases should be contained within inverted commas as shown. Make sure students are aware of this.

Worksheet 4.2

Noun + colour	Number of search engine 'hits'
"Navy blue"	_____
"Baby blue"	_____
"Sea blue"	_____
"Sky blue"	_____
"Banana yellow"	_____
"Canary yellow"	_____
"Olive green"	_____
"Lizard green"	_____
"Grass green"	_____
"Pea green"	_____
"Coal black"	_____
"Jet black"	_____

Photocopiable © Oxford University Press

Comment

Before carrying out activities such as these, it may be worthwhile finding out if any of your learners are colour blind. Standard tests can easily be found online.

4.3 Doubling pictures

Level Elementary +

Time 30 minutes

Aims To role play interviews with people who have accomplished interesting or strange feats.

Preparation

For this activity, you will need a few pictures of people who have accomplished interesting or strange feats. A copy of *Guinness World Records* would be perfect for this purpose, especially if you are willing to cut out the images which could then be laminated. There is also a selection of images from the book available at the *Guinness World Records* website (see Appendix 7b, page 133). Here are some examples of the type of images you could use:

- Lee Redmond, the owner of the longest fingernails in the world
- Ashrita Furman, who walked 130.3 km with a bottle of milk balanced on his head

- Jackie Bibby, who held eight rattlesnakes in his mouth by their tails for 12.5 seconds.

Procedure

1 Tell your students about the *Guinness World Records*. Show them a copy if possible and tell them that people will often go to extraordinary lengths to appear in it.

2 Show students the images one by one and in each case ask them to guess what records the individuals hold. Write key language on the board as it arises.

Example *She has the longest fingernails in the world.*
He walked 130.3 km with a bottle of milk balanced on his head.
He held 8 rattlesnakes in his mouth.

3 Put the pictures up around the classroom walls. Label the pictures with the names of the people in them.

4 Ask students to walk around the gallery in pairs and write down questions that they would ask if they could meet the individuals in the pictures. Ask them to write a minimum number of questions for each picture (two or three, for example) and offer grammatical support during this process.

Example *How long have you been growing your nails?*
Why did you decide to grow them?
Is it uncomfortable for you to sleep?
Do people stare at you in the street?
Is it difficult for you to peel an orange?

5 Tell students that they are now going to interview the people in the pictures. Place a chair underneath one of the pictures on the wall and ask for a volunteer to sit in it.

6 Ask students to direct all of their questions to the person in the picture and ask the volunteer sitting in the chair to answer in any way that he or she wants. As the interview progresses, encourage students to improvise by asking any new questions that they think of.

7 Repeat this process for all of the pictures.

Variation

Virtually any picture of a person can be doubled (see comment below) in the same way. Here are some more ideas:

- famous self-portraits (see Appendix 8c, page 134): ask your students to interview well-known artists. This can be a good way to engage students with any reading activity in which they find out about an artist's life and work for themselves (see Activity 2.2, for example).
- mug shots (i.e. police booking photographs such as the one in Activity 2.5; see Appendix 7i, page 134): these allow students to take on the role of interviewer using direct *wh*-questions.
- pictures of celebrities (see Appendix 8b, page 134): allow your students to be chat show hosts and interview the celebrities that they love or hate.

Comment

The process of providing a voice on behalf of a protagonist is often called 'doubling', a term that comes from psychodrama.

4.4 The bigger picture

Level Elementary +

Time 30 minutes

Aims To look at parts of an image and identify what they are, using *looks like*, *could be*, etc. To hypothesize on the content of the full picture, using present continuous, *there is*, etc.

Preparation

1 For this activity, you will need two pictures in which interesting things are happening.

2 Make a copy of each picture using a scanner, printer, or photocopier.

3 With a metal ruler and a paper-cutting knife, strategically cut out a few key pieces from each picture (see below) and laminate them if possible. Those below come from the images used in Activities 3.8 and 3.9.

Procedure

1 Write the following on the board:

It's …
It looks like …
It could be …

2 Ask your students to form a circle around you. Mix up the picture pieces and pass them around, one at a time. Ask students if they can identify what they see in each case. Offer linguistic support and encourage students to use the phrases you have written on the board whenever necessary. Write any new words on the board.

Example *What is this?*
It's a woman. It looks as if she's being attacked.
It looks like a sporting event/It's a crowd of people.
I think he's a policeman/He could be trying to help the woman.

3 Once you have discussed each picture piece, lay them all face up on a table.

4 Tell your students that the pieces have been taken from two different pictures. Ask students to divide the pieces into two piles, one for each picture. Let them reach agreement and don't correct them at this stage.

5 Divide the class into two groups. Give the first pile of picture pieces to group A and the second pile to group B. Tell students that they are detectives and their task is to work together to decide exactly what is going on in their pictures. Tell them that just like real detectives, they should hypothesize and use their imaginations to build up the full picture in their minds.

6 Circulate between the two groups and offer linguistic support as students reconstruct their pictures verbally and make notes about their group's theory.

7 Groups should then swap their sets of picture pieces and repeat steps 6 and 7 for their new pictures.

8 Pair up members from group A with members from group B and ask them to share their different ideas.

9 Select a student randomly, show him or her the first intact picture and ask him or her to describe it to the rest of the class. Choose a different student to do the same with the second picture. Finally show everyone the original pictures.

Variation

This type of activity can also be done with jigsaws.

Comment

This activity could be used as a follow-up to Activities 1.1, 2.2, or 4.2, which aim to equip students with the language they will need to talk about what is happening in pictures (present continuous, *there is/are*, etc.).

4.5 Name the group

Level Elementary +

Time 30–45 minutes, depending on the number of images obtained.

Aims To look at a series of images and guess what they have in common.

Preparation

Photo-sharing sites (see Appendix 2, page 130) can be host to a large number of diverse interest groups whose members upload and comment on photographs which are based around a particular theme (dogs, cityscapes, black and white photography, etc.). There are many groups with themes that are unusual, funny, or interesting. Here are some examples of the type of thing that can be found:

- people jumping
- people watching television
- numbers (bar codes, street numbers, car registrations, etc.) which are divisible by nine (see example opposite)
- green things
- animals staring at the camera
- dogs dressed up
- rude fruit and vegetables
- meals that people have prepared (recipes often included)
- photographs taken from cameras that have been thrown in the air (sometimes called 'camera tossing')
- objects that people carry in their handbags
- photographs taken from the air by cameras that have been attached to kites ('Kite Aerial Photography').

For this activity, you will need to go to a photo-sharing site (see Appendix 2, page 130) and search for a few interesting groups. For each group that you find, download about six images from it and arrange all images into a slide show (see Appendix 3, page 131).

Procedure

1   Find out if your students are aware of the phenomenon of online photo-sharing. If you have access to the Internet in class, show them around a photo-sharing website and show them some of the mainstream groups—themes such as wildlife photography, pictures of babies, underwater photography, etc.

2   Tell students that you have identified a number of interesting or unusual groups on the photo-sharing site. Tell them that you have downloaded a few images from each one and that you are going to use these for the basis of a game.

3   Write the following on the board:

    Does it have something to do with …?
    It could/might be …
    I think that they are photographs of …
    It can't be … because …

4   Tell students that their task is to try to work out the group's theme by looking at the photographs. Show the first photograph and ask for suggestions which you should write on the board.

5   Show the remaining photographs. After each one, ask students to continue guessing the theme of the group. Encourage them to use the language that was written on the board whenever necessary.

Example   *Does it have something to do with transport?*
It could/might be photographs of road signs.
I think that they are photographs of numbers.

As students see more pictures, they will have to change their ideas. Continue to offer help with language production and write up any new or useful vocabulary on the board.

6   Once students have seen the last photograph from the series, ask everyone to come to a final decision on the group's theme and ask them to write these down. Students may ask you to go through the slide show a second time.

7 Ask students to tell you about their decisions and give a point to everyone that was correct.

8 Repeat this process for the other series of photographs that you have prepared and add up all of the points at the end to find out who the winner is.

Follow-up

Online photo-sharing groups usually post a set of rules or guidelines on their home pages. Use cut and paste functions to create a worksheet that contains a selection of rules from the different groups that you look at in this activity. Ask your students to match the rules with the groups. Alternatively, students could predict a group's rules before reading them.

4.6 I don't know what you call it but …

Level Elementary +

Time 30–40 minutes

Aims To describe objects and talk about their function.

Preparation

On the way to your teaching venue, use your mobile phone or digital camera to take a number of pictures of objects that you don't know the names for in your students' language (street sign, post box, car registration plate, lamppost, etc.).

Procedure

1 Tell your students that you need their help: You want them to teach you some new words from their own language. Tell them that you are going to describe an object and you want them to listen and write down what they think it is (i.e. no shouting out).

2 Describe the first picture.

Example *This object is made of metal or plastic. You would find it attached to the front and back of every car. It has numbers and letters on it and is used to identify the car and, more importantly, its owner.*

During the process, write any useful or new language on the board.

Example *It's made of …*
You would find it …
It's used to …
It's used for …

3 Once you have finished each description, let your students compare their answers before letting them see the photograph. This process could be done as a quiz.

4 Put students into pairs. Each pair has to think of an object or two that they don't know the word for in English, make a quick drawing of it, and then prepare a description which will be read out to the class. For a model, they will be able to refer to the language that you have already written on the board.

Variation

If your students have mobile phones with cameras, they could be allowed out of the classroom for five minutes to find objects to photograph for step 4.

Comment

This activity works best with a monolingual class in a foreign country when you have some knowledge of their language.

4.7 A personal picture

Level Elementary +

Time This activity proceeds over two days and includes homework.
DAY 1 set task (10 minutes)
DAY 2 students give informal talks (5 minutes per talk)

Aims To prepare and give an informal talk about a personal photograph.

Preparation

1 Choose a photograph that you took yourself—one which is important to you in some way. Prepare a short written text that explains the background to it and why you chose it.

I took this photograph just outside my flat one summer about 2 years ago. I was sitting having a drink on the terrace of my local bar and there was a little dirty dog that wanted to be my friend. I had my camera and I wanted to take a picture of it but the problem was that it kept coming up too close to me and wanting to lick me so I had no space to take the photo. Eventually, I ran away from it and waited for it to catch up with me. Just before it got to me I took the picture. I had to use the flash since the sun was shining behind it. I chose this photograph because I like dogs and I think this one has a funny face.

2 Make photocopies of your photograph and text for your students.

Procedure

Day 1

1 Show students your photograph and tell them about it. Do not read from your prepared text—just talk naturally. Encourage students to interact by asking questions.

2 Tell students that you want them to prepare similar talks at home. Ask them to choose a personal photograph and prepare a talk which includes the following:

- When and where did you take the photograph?
- What were you doing when you took the photograph?
- Who are the people or animals in the picture?
- Is there any technical photographic information you would like to share?
- Why do you like it?

Write these points on the board.

3 Give students copies of your picture and prepared text. Ask them to identify the parts of the text that contain the information that you wrote on the board. Also ask students to identify grammatical features that they are going to use (past tenses, *there was/were*, etc.).

4 Ask students to prepare their talks by making extensive notes. Make sure they realize that they will have to bring their photographs into class along with their texts the next day.

Day 2

1 Ask students who have done their homework to present their photographs to the rest of the class. Encourage them not to read from their notes but to talk naturally as if they were showing the photograph to a friend.

2 Encourage listeners to interact by asking questions.

3 Put copies of students' work on the walls.

Variation 1

Rather than preparing talks at home, let students bring their photographs into class and talk about them to a partner. The partner can write notes and keywords and both students can then work together to organize these into a coherent text.

Variation 2

More and more people seem to carry around collections of photographs on their mobile phones. This means that you may actually have the material with you in the classroom and the activity does not have to proceed over two days.

Variation 3

Use a Dictaphone or similar recording device to record your own talk during step 1 (day 1). Step 3 (day 1) can then become a listening activity.

Follow-up

Scan your students' photographs and record their talks using a digital dictaphone (or similar device). If you have video-editing software (which often comes as standard on PCs or Macs), you could then make clips in which the stationary photograph occupies the full screen and the student's commentary is heard in the background. Clips like these can be uploaded on to video-sharing sites.

Comments

Showing your photographs to others is a very natural and communicative process. It can be a great activity for small or one-to-one classes. On Monday mornings, follow the question *What did you do at the weekend?* with *Did anyone take any photos on their mobile phone that they can show us?* Finally, if you use personal anecdotes for dictogloss activities (see Activity 1.5), it can be a good idea to find personal photographs to accompany them.

4.8 What were you doing?

Level Elementary +

Time 60 minutes

Aims To recall personal experiences and memories of the millennium.

Preparation

There is no preparation required for this activity.

Procedure

1 Show students the image below and ask them the following questions:

- *Can you identify the people in the picture?*
- *When and where do you think it was taken?*
- *Do you know what they are doing?*

2 Ask students how (and when) New Year is traditionally celebrated in their countries.

3 Tell students how you celebrated the millennium and then ask them to do the same (they can be put into pairs or groups for this speaking activity).

4 Ask students if they can recall and describe any well-known millennium images from their own media.

Variation

A similar activity can be done using images from September 11, 2001. Ask students to recall and describe as many images as possible from that day before asking them to talk about their own personal experiences, memories, and recollections of the day.

Follow-up

Ask students to write out their memories of the millennium in the style of a diary entry. Students can also do this for their recollections of the terrorist attacks of September 11, 2001 (see variation above).

Comment

The photo shows Queen Elizabeth II, British Prime Minister Tony Blair, and his wife Cherie Blair singing 'Auld Lang Syne' during the Millennium New Year celebrations on December 31, 1999 at the Millennium Dome in Greenwich, London

4.9 Flags in context

Level Elementary +

Time 30 minutes

Aims To discuss the different situations and contexts in which a symbol can be used.

Preparation

1 Using an image search engine (see Appendix 1, page 129), find a number of images in which flags appear in diverse situations.

Example
- Stars and Stripes on the moon
- flag being burnt
- flag draped over coffins
- flags being used by sports fans
- flags in fashion (for example, the Brazilian flag appears on a well-known brand of flip-flops)
- flags being used by political parties or social movements
- flags being used in association with royalty (for example, the Royal Standard flies over Buckingham Palace when the monarch is in residence)
- flags being raised over the podium after medal presentation at the Olympics
- flag on Mount Everest
- flag tattoos
- flag being flown half-mast

2 Use these images to create a slide show (see Appendix 3, page 131) and decide how you are going to display it (computer, projector, whiteboard, etc).

Procedure

1 Show students your country's flag and tell them everything you know about it. Here is how the Union Jack is made up:

2 Ask students to tell you or each other what they know about other national flags starting with those of their own countries. Ask them to consider colour, design, symbolism, etiquette, history, etc.

Example *The flag of Saudi Arabia is never flown at half-mast.*
The red disc on the flag of Bangladesh represents the blood of those who died for the country's independence.
The round object on the Portuguese flag (the armillary sphere) was an important navigational instrument for Portuguese sailors.
The flag of Libya is the only national flag that consists of only one colour.

If you have access to the Internet in class, pictures of flags can be found using an image search engine (see Appendix 1, page 129). Alternatively, ask students to draw them with colour pencils.

3 Tell students that you have some images of flags being used in different ways or appearing in different situations. Ask them to predict as many of these as possible (you may have to show students an image or two to start them off).

4 Show the images and for each one ask your students what they think is happening and how the flag is being used symbolically. Use the images as springboards for discussion by asking questions about them.

Example *Can you think of any situations in which a flag was flown at half mast? What do you think of people who paint their faces with their country's colours for international sporting events?*

5 Ask students to think of more situations. Can they think of different ways in which their own countries' flags are used?

Variation 1

Most of the example situations given above involve national flags. There are also situations in war, sport, etc. that can be used.

Example
- In war, waving a white flag signals surrender.
- During the closing ceremony of the Olympic Games, the Olympic Flag is passed to a representative of the next host country.
- Flags are used to communicate to drivers in motor racing. For example, yellow indicates caution, white indicates one lap to go, a black and white chequered flag indicates the end of the race.
- Flags are used to communicate swimming conditions on beaches.
- Flags are particularly important at sea. As well as flying its own national maritime flag, a ship in foreign waters should also display the flag of the country it is visiting (this is known as a courtesy flag). Failure to do this can be an indication of aggression.

Variation 2

Put up pictures of flags around the classroom walls and ask students to identify and label them with the countries or nations that they represent. As a listening activity, describe a flag and ask everyone to identify it by writing down the country.

Example *This flag consists of three vertical strips of colour: green on the left, red on the right, and white in the middle. In the middle of the white strip, there is an eagle standing on a cactus with a snake in its mouth.* (Mexico)

Follow-up

This activity can be good for building up linguistic awareness. Point out to your learners that words (both spoken and written) are like flags. They are symbols that can have different meanings in different contexts.

Comment

The photograph is of Norwegian explorer, Captain Roald Amundsen, taking sights at the South Pole with the Norwegian flag, 1911.

4.10 Film scenes

Level Pre-intermediate +

Time 20 minutes

Aims To recall and talk about scenes from films.

Preparation

There is no preparation required for this activity.

Procedure

1 Show your students the film still below and find out if anyone can name the film (*Dr Strangelove*).

2 If anyone in the class has seen the film, ask them if they can tell you what is happening. If no one has seen the film, ask them to guess who the men are and what is going on.

The image is taken from *Dr Strangelove* (directed by Stanley Kubrick in 1964). The US president (played by Peter Sellers) makes a 'friendly phone call' to the Soviet Premier to let him know that a disobedient United States Air Force commander has ordered a full-scale nuclear attack on Russia. The Russian ambassador (played by Peter Bull) is on the left hand side listening in on the call.

3 After discussing the famous scene from *Dr Strangelove*, tell students that you would like them to recall as many other films or TV programmes as possible that contain memorable phone calls (these

should not be restricted to productions in English, of course). Make a list of titles on the board and ask students to recall details of the plot, the phone call, the actors, etc. Some other possibilities include:

- *Dial M for Murder* (the 11.00 p.m. phone call which is central to the plot)
- *Scream* (the sinister phone call to Drew Barrymore in the opening scene)
- *Silence of the Lambs* (Hannibal Lecter's phone call to Clarice Starling from the Bahamas at the end of the film)
- *The Simpsons* (any prank phone call that Bart Simpson makes to Moe's Tavern).

For larger classes, students can be put into small groups for this task. Importantly, remind students not to spoil the endings of films for those who have not seen them.

4 If you have online access in class, you could use image search engine and video-sharing sites to find posters, stills, and trailers for the films that your students mention.

Variation 1

A film still, such as the one from *Dr Strangelove*, can be enough to bring a film that everyone has seen and enjoyed back into students' minds and give rise to discussion. Find out which stills to choose by talking to your students about their favourite films beforehand. After obtaining a selection of suitable stills (see comment below and Appendix 6, page 132) prepare some good questions to accompany them.

Example *What is the name of this film?*
What is it about?
What are the characters talking about in this scene?
What sort of relationship do the characters have?
What happened before this scene/what happens next?
What other films have the actors been in? Tell us about them.
What other films has the director made? Tell us about them.

Variation 2

Rather than asking students to recall memorable phone calls, ask them to think of as many films and TV programmes as possible containing any of the following:

- well-known scenes in restaurants and bars (e.g. the 'tipping dilemma' in *Reservoir Dogs*)
- famous love scenes (e.g. in *Some Like it Hot*)
- job interviews (e.g. Spud's disastrous effort in *Trainspotting*)
- people meeting for the first time (e.g. Billy Crystal and Meg Ryan in *When Harry met Sally*)
- people saying goodbye (e.g. Humphrey Bogart and Ingrid Bergman in *Casablanca*).

Follow-up

Film scripts can often be found online. Print off the dialogue for one of the scenes discussed in step 3 and obtain a film still for the scene in question (see comments below). Students will then be able to 'double' the picture (i.e. supply the voices for the people in the picture—see Activity 4.3) and act out the scene. Real time 'doubling' can also be done by playing a film clip with the sound turned down and asking students to synchronize their lines with the actors' lip movements.

Comment

Film stills can be obtained by taking photographs of your television screen while the DVD or video is paused at the correct place. Alternatively, play a DVD on your computer, pause it at the correct place, and use the screen capture function to save the image (see Appendix 6, page 132). See Appendix 7c, page 133 for more ideas on obtaining film images.

4.11 Controversial art

Level Pre-intermediate +

Time 45 minutes

Aims To describe controversial art. To express opinions.

Preparation

A piece of art can be controversial for many reasons. For example, it can:

- violate our own definitions of what art really is
- be obscene
- be seen as desecrating
- be seen as being beyond comprehension
- be deemed unethical
- be sold for a seemingly extortionate amount of money.

For this activity, you will need to select a number of images of controversial artwork (see Appendix 7d, page 133). Put these around the classroom walls if possible or arrange as a slide show if not (see Appendix 3, page 131). Please note that some of the images mentioned below can be considered quite offensive in some cultures and should be avoided in such cases.

Example
- Lucian Freud's portrait of the Queen (criticized as being unflattering)
- Marcel Duchamp: *Fountain* (a porcelain urinal signed 'R Mutt')
- Chris Ofili: *No woman no cry* (This painting by the 1998 Turner Prize-winner stands on two dried varnished lumps of elephant dung. A third piece is used as the pendant of the necklace that hangs around the subject's neck.)
- Tracey Emin: *My bed* (controversial piece shortlisted for the 1999 Turner Prize)

- Damien Hirst: *The Physical Impossibility of Death in the Mind of Someone Living* (a shark preserved in a tank of formaldehyde)
- Anything by Yves Klein (his bizarre performance art can be seen on video-sharing sites.)
- Any image from *Body Worlds*
- Any painting by Jackson Pollock
- A photograph of any piece of work by Christo and Jeanne-Claude (for example, *Wrapped Coast* in which they covered an Australian cliff-lined shore with one million square feet of light beige fabric)
- Photographs of well-known, controversial public art and architecture

Number the pieces on display and prepare a worksheet such as Worksheet 4.11 for the number of artworks you are showing. Make a copy for each student.

Procedure

1 Find out if your students know anything about the pieces of art that you have selected.

2 Give out copies of the worksheet and ask your students to complete it as they go around the gallery (or see the slide show).

3 Mingle with your students as they carry out their task and take a note of pairs of students who have opposite opinions about specific pieces. For example, if Juan likes Lucian Freud's portrait of the Queen but Nuria hates it, make a note of this.

4 Ask everyone to sit down and review the pieces one by one. Set up debates by singling out student pairs who you know disagree.

5 The definition of the word 'art' may come on trial during this activity. Ask your students to write down their own definitions of what art is and then compare them.

Worksheet 4.11	Do you like it?	If you don't like it, say why.
Artwork 1 Artist's name Year it was created Any other relevant information	Yes/No	
Artwork 2 Artist's name Year it was created Any other relevant information	Yes/No	
Artwork 3 Artist's name Year it was created Any other relevant information	Yes/No	
Artwork 4 Artist's name Year it was created Any other relevant information	Yes/No	

Photocopiable © Oxford University Press

Variation

Controversial public art is often good for stirring up reactions in people. Take photographs of local pieces of graffiti, advertising billboards, and buildings and sculptures which polarize opinion. Let your students share their thoughts by deciding whether they see each piece as being 'decoration or desecration' and explain their reasons. See Activity 4.1 for more ideas.

Follow-up 1

Many thought-provoking art quotations can be found in quotations books and online.

Example
- 'A mere copier of nature can never produce anything great.' (Sir Joshua Reynolds)
- 'Art does not reproduce what is visible; rather, it makes things visible.' (Paul Klee)

- 'It's clever, but is it art?' (Rudyard Kipling)
- 'Rules and models destroy genius and art.' (William Hazlitt)

Obtain a few of these, dictate them to your students, and ask them to consider if any of them can be applied to the work on display in the classroom.

Follow-up 2

Ask your students if they can think of any controversial art or artists from their own backgrounds. Use an image search engine (see Appendix 1, page 129) to find pictures and ask your learners to tell you about them.

4.12 Celebrities

Level   Pre-intermediate +

Time   30 minutes

Aims   To use images of celebrities from students' own countries to seed discussion. To share opinions about the personalities in question.

Preparation

Obtain a selection of images of well-known personalities from your learners' own culture. If you are working abroad, look in local newspapers or magazines for pictures of musicians, pop stars, artists, television presenters, actors, politicians, sports players, and any personalities of the moment. You could even use a camera to capture shots of celebrities on television screens. If you are not working abroad, you could ask students to find pictures themselves and bring them into class.

Procedure

1 Tell your students that you would like to know more about their country's pop culture and media.

2 Lay out all the pictures on a table or on the floor so that students can see them.

3 Ask students to choose two pictures each—one of a celebrity they like and one of a celebrity they dislike.

4 Let students take it in turn to tell you about the celebrities they have chosen and find out if other students share the same opinions.

Variation 1

Ask your students to explain political cartoons from their own press. Ask them about the background events, politicians involved, issues concerned, etc. Alternatively, try the same thing with well-known historical photographs from learners' cultures.

Variation 2

They say that everybody has a 'claim to fame'—a connection or link to a famous person (e.g. 'Sean Connery used to live on the same street as my grandparents.'). Take in a picture of the famous person to whom you have a claim, regardless of how distant it may be. Explain the term 'claim to fame', tell students about yours, and ask them to tell you about theirs. Ask them to find images of the famous people in question using an image search engine if possible (see Appendix 1, page 129).

Comments

1 Since one of the best ways of learning about a new country's media, politics, or pop culture can be through students, this activity can work well for language teachers who have recently moved abroad.

2 The photo is of Bollywood star Govinda being congratulated by supporters after winning the seat for the north Bombay constituency.

4.13 How do you feel?

Level Pre-intermediate +

Time 60 minutes

Aims To talk about situations which are exhausting, boring, relaxing, confusing, etc. To act out the corresponding adjectives of emotions (*exhausted, bored, relaxed, confused*, etc).

Preparation

1 Use sheets of A4 paper and a marker pen to prepare eight large adjective labels like the ones shown in the photographs below. Prepare one for each of the following adjectives:

- *exhausted*
- *bored*
- *relaxed*
- *confused*
- *annoyed*
- *frightened*
- *embarrassed*
- *disappointed*

2 Take a digital camera into class.

Clockwise from top left: *Tired and exhausted, bored, relaxed, confused, annoyed, frightened, embarrassed, disappointed.*

Procedure

1 Write the following questions on the board and ask students to copy them.

What is your pet hate?
Can you recall a time when you felt absolutely exhausted?
For you, what would be the most boring job in the world?
What are your phobias?
What do you do to relax?
What do you think is the most confusing aspect of the English language?
Can you recall an embarrassing incident?
What is the most disappointing, over-rated, or predictable film you have ever seen?

2 Go over the questions and explain any unknown language.

Example   *A 'pet hate' is something trivial that people do which annoys you a lot. When you are embarrassed, your face goes red.*

3 For each question, give students an answer of your own.

Example   *My pet hate is when people stand side-by-side and block the escalator in the underground.*

4 Put students into pairs and ask them to discuss the questions. While students are speaking, circulate among pairs, listen in, offer linguistic support, and take a note of any good answers that you hear.

5 Once students have finished, encourage individuals to share their answers with the rest of the class and write any new or useful language on the board. After each question has been discussed and explored in full, choose a student (perhaps one with a particularly good answer) and give him or her the appropriate adjective sheet. Ask the student to hold it up and act out the emotion written on it. Take a photograph in each case.

Example Teacher: *So, your pet hate is people who throw litter on the street. That makes you annoyed. OK, now I want you to look annoyed for the camera.*
Teacher: *You suffer from vertigo. You are frightened of heights. Can you look frightened for the camera?*

Follow-up 1

Before the next day, use an image application (see Appendix 4, page 131) to cover up the adjectives on each photograph. Duplicate the photographs first so that you can create a slide show (see Appendix 3, page 131) of image pairs that look like this:

Show students the images with the words hidden and ask them to recall the adjectives. This can be a good opportunity to practise the structure *look* + adjective.

Example *I think she looks tired.*

With your students' permission, use the slide show to introduce this language to other classes.

Follow-up 2

Digital cameras are ideal for documenting the vocabulary and language that arise in the classroom. Simply write the date on a corner of the board and take a picture of it at the end of the class. For the activity described above, this method could be used to record the vocabulary that arises in step 5. Later, refer to the photograph and write out sentences which can be dictated to your students at the beginning of the next lesson for revision.

Example *Chiara is scared of getting stuck in a lift.*
Paola gets annoyed when people jump the queue.
Antonella gets annoyed when pictures on the wall aren't straight.
Monica would get bored if she worked in a bank.

Follow-up 3

Ask students to write up their answers. Along with the photographs, put these on a class blog (see Appendix 2, page 130).

Comment

If you intend to photograph your students, you must consider their privacy and obtain their permission. Most people are unenthusiastic about having a camera thrust into their face, especially if it is first thing on a Monday morning. If possible, give prior warning of your intentions. That way, at least, everyone will have the opportunity to make themselves look good on the day should they want to. Alternatively, use your discretion and focus in on the extroverts and shy away from those who may feel self-conscious. If you intend to photograph young learners, you *must* get permission from parents first.

4.14 Where in the world?

Level Intermediate +

Time 30–45 minutes, depending on the number of images obtained.

Aims To look at pictures from all over the world and decide where they were taken. To use images as a springboard for discussion.

Preparation

Prepare a classroom gallery of images from around the world (see Appendix 7a, page 133). Look for pictures of:

- places
- cityscapes
- aerial photographs
- satellite pictures
- local people
- pictures of the aftermath of natural disasters.

Procedure

1 As your students enter the classroom, invite them to walk around the gallery and think about where in the world the various pictures were taken.

2 Put your students into pairs or small groups and ask them to share and compare ideas about each image. It would be a good idea to have an atlas available during this step.

3 During this discussion step, you could draw attention to the following structures by writing them on the board:

It looks like …
It could be …
It can't be …

4   Finally, tell students about the images one at a time. Tell them about the content of the picture and where and when it was taken, and give them any other relevant background information. In each case, do not let students know which picture you are referring to. Allow them to look around the room and decide (silently) which one you are talking about.

Variation 1

Prepare a short explanatory text for each picture that is being used or, even better, obtain them from the source magazines, newspapers, calendars, or books. These can be exploited during step 4. Rather than doing the talking yourself, give each student a text, ask him or her to identify which image it refers to, and finally ask students to present their images to the rest of the class.

Variation 2

Use your own personal photographs to create a gallery of all the places you have been to in your life. Invite your learners to bring in their own pictures and do the same. Find out exactly which countries in the world your students have been to and which ones they would like to go to.

Follow-up

Ask each student to choose a country or city and use it as the basis for a project, poster, or presentation. If you decide to use pictures such as the one above, students could choose to look into one of the natural disasters illustrated.

Comment

The photograph shows an Acehnese man looking at a boat left on top of a house as a result of the tsunami in the Indonesian provincial city of Banda Aceh on February 24, 2005. Almost 240,000 people are dead or missing and more than 400,000 were made homeless in Aceh by the December 26, 2004 tsunami.

4.15 Yesterday's news

Level Intermediate +

Time 45 minutes

Aims To discuss the news by talking about pictures taken from the previous day's newspaper.

Preparation

1 Obtain a copy of the previous day's newspaper. It is important that the paper comes from the country in which you and your students live. It does not have to be in English.

2 Cut out a number of images that relate to the most important or interesting news stories from the previous day. Put these up on the walls around the classroom.

Procedure

1 Put students into pairs and give them a few minutes to look at the pictures on the wall and decide why they were in yesterday's newspaper.

2 Take all the images off the wall and ask everyone to sit around in a circle. Go through the images one by one, discuss the news stories, and share opinions.

Variation 1

Add a competitive edge to the activity by turning it into a quiz (there is no need to put the pictures on the wall for this). Divide the class into two teams. The teams take it in turn to be shown an image and say why it featured in the previous day's news. Award points in any way you feel is appropriate.

Variation 2

Many popular online newspapers have a daily selection of images from around the world (see Appendix 7e, page 133). Each image will be accompanied by a short text—often just a single sentence. Download a selection of the day's international images (ten would be a suitable number). Use cut and paste functions to create a document which contains all of the mini explanatory texts and make copies of these for your students. Their reading task is to match the texts with the images.

Follow-up 1

Ask students each to choose a different story and find out more about it online. They can then report their findings back to the rest of the class.

Follow-up 2

Students could translate any short story from a newspaper in their language into English. This could then be compared with the equivalent story in English, for example from an online newspaper.

4.16 The Olympics

Level   Intermediate +

Time   60 minutes

Aims   To look at and talk about symbols and icons associated with the Olympic Games.

Preparation

Make photocopies of Worksheet 4.16 for your students.

Worksheet 4.16

1 Match the icons with the sports/events.

1 _f_   2 ___   3 ___   4 ___

5 ___   6 ___   7 ___   8 ___

9 ___   10 ___   11 ___

a Fencing   e Cycling   i Hurdling
b Swimming   f Football   j Judo
c Archery   g Badminton   k Shooting
d Weightlifting h Sprinting   l Javelin

2 Imagine you have just invented a new sport or event that is going to be introduced into the Olympics. On a separate piece of paper, do the following:

- write out the main rules or describe the objectives of your new Olympic sport/event
- decide what it is going to be called
- create an icon in the style of the ones above for your new sport/event.

Photocopiable © Oxford University Press

Procedure

1 Show students the poster below and draw their attention to the five rings.

2 Ask students the following questions.

What do the five rings represent? (the five main continents of the world)

Can you name the continents? (The Americas are included as one and Antarctica is excluded. Specific continents are not represented by specific rings.)

Is a ring usually a positive or a negative symbol? (In most cultures, rings are usually positive symbols.)

What can a ring symbolize? (eternity, love, strength, harmony, etc.)

If a ring is being worn, what does it mean depending on where it is being worn and who is wearing it? (e.g. the different fingers, toes, navel, man, woman, etc.)

Do you think that a ring is a good icon to represent a continent? Why?

What is symbolized by the fact that the rings are interlocking? (eternal unity and harmony between the nations of the world?)

The above image is in black and white but can you tell what colours the rings should be? (left to right: blue, yellow, black, green, red)

Along with white (the Olympic flag background colour) do you know what the 4.16
different colours represent? (They are the colours that appeared on all
the national flags at the time when the symbol was designed.)

3 Ask your students if they like the Olympic Games. Ask them where
they originated, where the last ones were held, where the next ones
are being held, etc.

4 Ask students to think of as many Olympic sports/events as possible
that end with the letters *-ing*. After a few suggestions, give them
Worksheet 4.16 and ask them to complete question 1. For those
that do not end in *-ing*, they should decide whether to use *playing*
or *doing*.

Answers: 1f 2d 3g 4c 5b 6k 7i 8j 9l 10h 11a 12e
Playing is used with games (football, badminton) and *doing* with
activities (archery, judo, javelin).

5 Let students compare their answers with each other and ask them
what their favourite/least favourite Olympic sports/events are. Find
out which ones they have tried themselves.

6 See if everyone can remember all twelve sports/events just by
looking at the icons.

7 Ask your students to complete the second task on the worksheet.
Make sure that they understand the instructions. They may need
some inspiration for this task. See Variation below for one possible
idea.

8 Allow each student to present his or her icon to the rest of the class
who should try to decipher the nature of the new Olympic sport or
event.

Variation

The image manipulation contest site Worth1000 (see Appendix 7f,
page 133) has a series of image galleries called 'surreal sports'. There
are some very cleverly created pictures of people engaged in diverse
activities such as elephant boxing, fish throwing, and chicken
catching. Try using these to stimulate your learners' imagination
prior to step 8 (above).

Follow-up

Ask students to think of and describe as many other images as
possible that can be related to the Olympic Games. These could
include logos, mascots, advertisements, memorable TV moments,
stadiums, etc.

4.17 Photography competition

Level All levels

Time 30–40 minutes

Aims To judge a photography competition. To express opinions and preferences.

Preparation

In the age of digital photography and online image-sharing there has been a boom in the number of online photography competitions for amateurs and professionals alike (see Appendix 7f, page 133). In many cases, shortlisted entries will remain on the sites even after the competition is over. For this activity, find a competition that has already been judged, download a number of the photographs (12, for example), and arrange them as a slide show (see Appendix 3, page 131). Make sure you include the winners and runners up in your selection.

Procedure

1 Have the slide show playing on loop (repeatedly) as your students come into the classroom.

2 Tell your students about the photography competition that you have chosen and draw their attention to the slide show of entries. (You do not have to let students know that they will be seeing pictures from an old competition.)

3 Tell students to imagine that they are the competition judges. Ask everyone to note which photograph they would choose to be the winner and also which one they would choose for the runner-up.

4 Stop the slide show and ask students to tell the rest of the class about their choices—what they like about the photographs and why they think they should win. In each case, students will have to

identify the photographs by describing them briefly from memory. Write any new language that emerges on the board. For larger classes, put students into groups for this step.

5 Give a photograph two points each time it is chosen as a winner and one point each time it is chosen as a runner-up. Then add up the points and find out which picture has won the prize and which one has come second.

6 Tell students which pictures actually won and let them express their feelings of outrage at the injustice of it all.

Variation 1

Rather than displaying the images as a slide show, print them off and put them up on the classroom walls to create a photo gallery. Remove them from the wall before step 4.

Variation 2

This activity can also be used with entries from:

• students' own photographs (all pieces of work should be entered anonymously)
• images from a photo-sharing site (see Appendix 2, page 130) after selecting their favourite pictures, students can send friendly emails to the photographers to say why they like their pictures and also ask any questions that relate to them
• photo-manipulation contests (see Appendix 7f, page 133)
• art competitions
• advertising awards (see Appendix 7f, page 133)
• architecture and design awards.

Comment

The photograph is by Jeff Yonover and is entitled 'Rajan snorkelling'. This photograph came highly commended in the 2007 Gerald Durrell Award for Endangered Wildlife, part of the Shell Wildlife Photographer of the Year.

5
Flash images

Imagine a magic mirror that hangs on your classroom wall upon which you can call up pictures of anything you want. A Brazilian student is telling the rest of the class about a fruit from her country. It would be helpful if you could see it: You say, 'Magic mirror, show us a carambola,' and *POP* you suddenly realize that she's been talking about a star fruit.

The mirror in question is, of course, your computer screen. With Internet connection and an image search engine we really can call up pictures of virtually anything we want.

The first activity in this chapter aims to demonstrate to students the power and potential that this invaluable tool can provide for self study.

From flashcards to flash images

Image search engines allow teachers to create digital slide shows of thematically selected images to teach virtually any piece of grammar or lexis that learners require. Unlike picture flashcards that are often created specifically for the purpose of teaching, downloaded images are generally authentic and may be better for generating spontaneous, unplanned discussion.

As well as being digitally obtained, flash 'images' can also be digitally stored. A single gigabyte of memory can hold well over 10,000 downloaded images, conveniently allowing a teacher to carry an entire image collection into the classroom in his or her pocket. Furthermore, unlike tangible picture cards which are often quite small, the electronically displayed images which we flash at our learners can be as big as the display medium itself (computer screen, projector and screen, etc).

Most of the activities in this chapter aim to demonstrate how teachers may take advantage of the following popular technologies:

- image search engines (Appendix 1, page 129)
- digital slide shows (Appendix 3, page 131)
- image organizers (Appendix 4, page 131).

5.1 The world's biggest picture dictionary

Level All levels

Time 60 minutes

Aims To learn how to carry out an online image search. To promote autonomy of learning.

Preparation

1 Make a copy of Worksheet 5.1 on page 96 for each student.

2 If your teaching venue has a computer room where students (or pairs of students) can each have access to the Internet, reserve it for this activity. If not, set up a computer in your classroom with online access. An interactive whiteboard would be ideal but a normal computer will work as long as everyone can see the screen.

3 If you are not sure how to use an image search engine, familiarize yourself with the process using Appendix 1, page 129.

4 Have a good monolingual English learner's dictionary available (optional).

Procedure

1 Give out copies of Worksheet 5.1 and show your students that it contains ten pairs of nouns (*clock* and *watch*, *purse* and *wallet*, *wardrobe* and *cupboard*, *floor* and *ground*, etc.).

2 For each word pair, find out if anyone can explain the difference. For large classes, ask students to do this in pairs or small groups before asking for feedback.

3 Ask students if they know how to use an image search engine. Ask them which ones they use or which ones they have heard of.

4 Use a computer to demonstrate how to search for images of the first pair of words (*clock* and *watch*). Write up any useful or new language on the board as you go over/elicit the process.

   1 Go to the search engine.
   2 Click on 'Images'.
   3 Type in 'clock'.
   4 Click on 'Search'.

5 The multiple small images or 'thumbnails' that are displayed on the computer screen following an image search are more valuable than verbal descriptions of the words in question. Ask students to come to a consensus definition for each word based on what they see.

Example *Watch: A thing that you wear on your wrist for telling the time.*
Clock: A watch that goes on the wall or beside your bed.

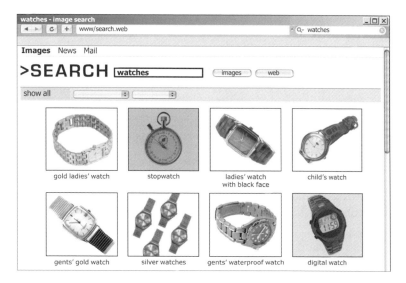

6 Ask students to write these definitions in the appropriate boxes on their worksheets.

7 Put students into pairs or small groups and ask them to complete the process of finding images and writing definitions based on what they see. Circulate and offer help with language and technological support if necessary (make use of the instructions that were written on the board during step 4 for this purpose). If you are not in a computer room, students can still work on their definitions in pairs or groups, but individuals should be given the opportunity to take control of the computer/interactive whiteboard to find images for the rest of the class to see.

8 Once everyone has completed their worksheets, let different student pairs or groups merge and share their definitions.

9 If you have a dictionary, read out or dictate definitions of each word.

Variation 1

If you do not have Internet access during class time, there are alternative options:

- Turn the activity into a homework exercise.
- Find and download images before class and arrange them into a slide show.
- Make slide shows of screen prints of search results (see Appendix 1, page 129).

Variation 2

This activity can also be done with:

- confusing verb or gerund pairs such as *carrying* and *wearing*, *washing* and *cleaning*, *spill* and *pour*, etc.
- false friends (pairs of words in two languages that look similar but differ in meaning). For example, Spanish students can be shown that *embarrassed* does not mean *embarazada* (pregnant) or that *soap* is not *sopa* (soup).

Worksheet 5.1

Clock	Watch
Purse	Wallet
Wardrobe	Cupboard
Floor	Ground
Pots	Pans
Stairs	Steps
Seat	Chair
Rug	Carpet
Road	Street
Pigeon	Dove

Photocopiable © Oxford University Press

If you have Internet access in class, an image search engine can be regarded as a powerful resource for consultation whenever the need arises. Such a tool can be useful for enhancing spontaneous classroom conversations, especially when students or teacher are trying to tell others about food, places, people, customs, or anything else from their countries, cultures, and backgrounds.

Comments

1 The image of a word or piece of language is an important part of its meaning. One of the aims of the activity outlined above is to demonstrate to learners that through the use of technology it is often more effective for them to see new words or items for themselves than to rely on teacher explanations.

2 In order to avoid unexpected rude surprises on your computer screen, make sure that the image search filter system is on. Filters are usually managed under user 'preferences'.

5.2 Picture word search

Level All levels

Time 15 minutes

Aims To revise vocabulary from a text.

Preparation

1 Select a text that your students have already studied.

2 Select a number of words from the text that you would like students to revise.

3 Enter each of the selected words into an image search and in each case scroll through the pages until you find an image which portrays or exemplifies the word in some way or another. Note that results of image searches are very unpredictable and virtually any item or word, whether it is a noun, verb, adjective, etc, may give rise to interesting and useful pictures. Here are seven examples of images that were obtained using individual words taken from Munch's diary entry (see Activity 2.3):

- a sunset (word entered = 'setting')
- a man holding his head in his hands (word entered = 'anxiety')
- the pause button on a DVD player (word entered = 'paused')
- a picturesque Norwegian fjord (word entered = 'fjord')
- the Leaning Tower of Pisa (word entered = 'leaned')
- Edvard Munch's 'The Scream' (word entered = 'scream')
- a path in a forest (word entered = 'path')

4 Save the images and arrange them as a slide show (see Appendix 3, page 131) in random order.

5 Decide how you are going to display the slide show in class (computer screen, projector, interactive whiteboard, portable media player, etc.).

Procedure

1 Show students the slide show and for each picture ask them to make notes to describe what they see. Do not offer any help with language at this point.

2 Refer students back to the original text and tell them that the images they have just seen were obtained by entering individual words or items from the text into a search engine. Ask students to work out which words were taken from the text and identify the images that they correspond to.

Variation 1

This activity can be done in reverse. While planning a reading or listening activity, look through the text for key words or items that you wish to pre-teach and find images for each one. Use the resulting slide show to teach the relevant vocabulary and ask students to predict what the text is about.

Variation 2

In Activity 4.13 (Follow-up 2), it is mentioned that digital cameras can be used to photograph the board and document the language that arises in the classroom during speaking activities. Make use of these 'records' to look for images of words and items that you want to revise.

5.3 Noun marriages

Level Elementary +

Time 20 minutes

Aims To use images to learn about collocations involving noun pairs.

Preparation

1 In English, nouns often associate to form distinct lexical items (*cowboy*, *alarm clock*, *flower power*, *football*, *ice cream*, *birthday*, etc). For this activity, you will need about ten images in which items like these are represented.

Example
- a sunflower (e.g. Van Gogh's painting)
- a belly button
- a guide dog
- a sex symbol (e.g. Marilyn Monroe)
- a catwalk
- a bullfight
- a traffic jam
- a couch potato (someone who watches too much television)
- a bodybuilder
- a lighthouse

5.3

2 Save the images on to your computer's hard drive and prepare a slide show (see Appendix 3, page 130).

Procedure

1 Show your students the images and ask them to tell you what they see. If they do not know the correct names (*bodybuilder, guide dog, etc.*), encourage them to use their own words.

Example   *a person who spends too long in the gym*
a dog that helps a blind person

2 Write the constituent nouns on the board for students to copy. For example, if you are using the example images from above, write:

belly	*cat*	*guide*	*sex*
body	*couch*	*house*	*sun*
builder	*dog*	*jam*	*symbol*
bull	*fight*	*light*	*traffic*
button	*flower*	*potato*	*walk*

3 Show your students that these words can be paired and the resulting combinations will refer to the things that they saw in the slide show. Make sure they understand that every word must be used only once. Give an example or two to get them started.

Example   *guide + dog = guide dog*
sun + flower = sunflower

4 Have the slide show playing on repeat (i.e. on 'loop') so that everyone is given continuous access to the images. Ask students to pair up the remaining words. Let them work in pairs or small groups if they want to.

5 Let students mingle and compare their answers. They may produce some amusing word combinations (e.g. *a jam potato, a belly builder*).

6 Give students the answers and drill pronunciation of each one. Concentrate on the stress patterns. Note that when two nouns come together, the stress usually falls on the first. As will be seen in the next activity, this is exactly opposite to the stress pattern that is observed for adjective-noun pairs:

Noun–noun		Adjective–noun	
CAT walk	Oo	Yellow CARD	ooO
TRAffic jam	Ooo	Pink PANther	oOo
COUCH potato	Oooo	The red MAN	ooO

Variation

This activity can also be done using well-known examples of the possessive 's.

Example *Bird's nest* (the Beijing 2008 Olympic Stadium)
Adam's apple (colloquial name for the laryngeal prominence)
Charlie's Angels (a famous US television series)
Director's cut (an image of a DVD box, for example)
McDonald's restaurant
Levi's Jeans
Noah's Ark
Valentine's Day (a picture of a card, for example)

Remove the 's from each item and mix up the constituent nouns as before in step 2). Students' task will then be to pair up the nouns and add the 's in the correct place.

Comment

Students may want to know when a noun partnership results in a single new word (*tablecloth, wallpaper, bookshop*, etc.) or when the words remain detached (*table tennis, toilet paper, pet shop*). As the examples I have just given here demonstrate, it can be difficult to form a rule. Learners can be encouraged either not to worry too much about this point of convention or to consult a dictionary if in doubt.

5.4 What do you do with a didgeridoo?

Level Beginner to elementary

Time 45 minutes

Aims To practise present simple question forms.

Preparation

1 Use an online image search engine to find and download images of the following:

- a didgeridoo
- New York
- a polar bear (at the North Pole)
- someone playing table tennis
- a window cleaner
- a honey bee
- an anteater
- a dishwasher
- a bottle opener.

2 Arrange the images into a slide show (see Appendix 3, page 131) and decide how you are going to display them in class.

Procedure

1 Put your students into pairs or teams.

2 Tell them that they are going to have a quiz. Each question will be read out twice. Team members should confer and write down answers.

3 Ask the following questions:

What do you do with a didgeridoo?
Where does a New Yorker live?
Where do polar bears live?
What does a table tennis player play?
What does a window cleaner clean?
What do honey bees make?
What does an anteater eat?
What do you put in a dishwasher?
What do you open with a bottle opener?

4 Check answers and find out which pair or team has the most right.

5 Show students the slide show to clarify any confusion. For each image, elicit the question that was asked and drill it. If necessary, make use of your fingers to show students the individual words in each question.

6 Allow the slide show to play on repeat ('loop') and ask students to reconstruct the nine questions using the pictures as prompts. For beginners, you could write the following guide on the board:

Question word	Auxiliary	Subject	Verb	The rest of the question
What	do	you	do	with a didgeridoo?
Where	does	a New Yorker	live?	—

5.5 Adjectives

Level Beginner to elementary

Time 30 minutes

Aims To learn some common adjectives. To learn that adjectives go before nouns. To examine stress patterns of adjective–noun pairs.

Preparation

1 For this activity, you will need about 16 images which represent adjective-noun pairs. For example, find and download pictures of any of the items below. Note that in each case, the image can usually be obtained by entering the words in inverted commas into the search window.

Example
- 'bare feet'
- 'Big Ben'
- 'fast food'
- 'identical twins'
- 'New York' (also known as the 'Big Apple')
- 'The Last Supper' (Leonardo da Vinci's painting)
- a 'best man'
- a 'German Shepherd' (also called an Alsatian)
- a 'Mexican wave'
- a 'Russian doll'
- a 'wet paint' sign
- a card that says 'Happy Birthday'
- a computer 'hard drive'
- a pair of 'high heels'
- a set of 'false teeth'

- an athlete competing in the 'long jump' or the 'high jump'
- the 'Wild West'
- the film poster for 'Dirty Dancing'
- the film poster for 'Pretty Woman'
- the film poster for 'Scary Movie'

2 Save the images on to your hard drive and arrange them as a slide show (see Appendix 3, page 131). Decide how the slide show is going to be displayed in class.

Procedure

1 Show your learners the slide show. For each image try to elicit what the subject is and try to involve students in any relevant discussion by asking questions.

Example *Has anyone been to New York?*
Who has seen this film? What is it about?
Has anyone ever taken part in a Mexican wave?

2 In each case, before moving on to the next image, drill the target language. Pay close attention to the stress patterns. Note that in adjective-noun pairs, stress usually falls on the noun. For example:

Adjective–noun	Stress pattern
Bare FEET	oO
Russian DOLL	ooO
Grand CANyon	oOo

There are some exceptions:

HARD drive	Oo
LONG jump	Oo

3 Pair up students or put them into small groups and ask them to remember and write down as many images as possible (you may want to go through the slide show a second time before you do this). Tell them how many images they saw so that they know their goal. Put a time limit on the activity and see who can recall the most.

4 Go over the answers and once again drill pronunciation of the target language paying attention to the stress patterns.

Variation 1

Include one adjective-noun pair in the slide show that is an exception to the stress pattern rule (see step 2 above). Ask students to listen to your own pronunciation of all the target language and identify which adjective-noun pair is different to the others.

Variation 2

This activity can be given a colour theme using images of any of the following:

- a 'black hole'
- a 'blue whale'
- a 'greyhound' (either a racing dog or the national US coach company)
- a copy of the 'Yellow Pages' directory

- a referee showing a football player a 'red card'
- a referee showing a football player a 'yellow card'
- a spoonful of 'brown sugar'
- the 'green man' (the pedestrian crossing signal light that means 'walk')
- the 'red man' (the pedestrian crossing signal light that means 'don't walk')
- the 'Pink Panther'
- the 'White House'
- 'Purple Rain' (a poster of the album by Prince or the film)

5.6 Bin, Ben, and Bean

Level Elementary +

Time 30 minutes

Aims To learn to distinguish three similar vowel sounds.

Preparation

1 For this activity, you will need to download images of things that when described will require the production of either the /ɪ/, /e/ or /iː/ vowel sound. To find images of the examples below, try entering the words in inverted commas into the search window of an image search engine.

The /ɪ/ vowel sound

- actor 'Will Smith'
- ex-US president 'Bill Clinton'
- a plate of 'fish and chips'
- a pair of 'kissing fish'
- a 'Christmas dinner'
- a 'lipstick'
- a 'windmill'

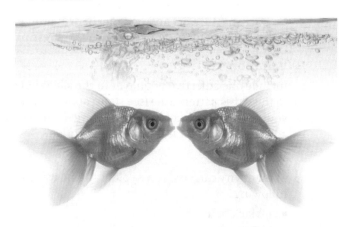

The /e/ vowel sound

- a 'best seller' (Harry Potter, for example)
- 'Elvis Presley'
- a 'redhead'
- someone eating 'breakfast in bed'
- a 'heavy metal' rock band
- Manchester United Football Club (aka 'the Red Devils')
- the film poster for 'X-men'

The /i:/ vowel sound

- any 'Greenpeace' image (the environmental campaigning organization)
- a 'Beefeater' (a Tower of London guard)
- 'Steven Spielberg and ET'
- a 'DVD'
- a 'queen bee'
- some 'green beans'
- some 'cream cheese'

2 Set up a slide show of the images you have selected (see Appendix 3, page 131). They should be ordered randomly.

Procedure

1 Write the following on the board and drill their sound.

1 Bin /ɪ/
2 Ben /e/
3 Bean /iː/

2 Say one of the three words and ask a student to identify it by giving you the corresponding number 1, 2, or 3. Repeat this several times with different students.

3 Change roles with your learners: Ask them to pronounce the words while you identify the sounds.

4 Tell your students that you are going to show them a Bin, Ben, and Bean slide show. In each case, in order to describe what they see, they will have to pronounce one of the three vowels in question.

5 Show students the images and, whenever possible, ask them to tell you what they see. For each image, drill pronunciation of the target language and ask students to identify which of the three vowel sounds is the prominent one.

6 Once you have completed the slide show, draw the following grid on the board and ask students to copy it into their notebooks.

Bin /ɪ/	Ben /e/	Bean /iː/

7 Ask students to recall the things they saw. Give everyone a chance to remember an item, go up to the board, and write it in the corresponding column. This time they will have to think about spelling as well as pronunciation. Also, encourage students to write the stress patterns beside the words: Breakfast in bed = oooO, etc.

8 Go through the slide show a second time to see if you missed out any of the images in the previous step and add these to the grid.

9 Put students into pairs. Ask them to look at all the items in the grid and try to work out spelling rules for each of the three sounds.

Example *The letter I is associated with the Bin sound.*
The letter E and the combination EA are associated with the Ben sound.
The combinations EE and EA are associated with the Bean sound.

Variation

This activity can be used to address any pair or triplet of confusing vowel sounds. Think of a few images that you can download for each one.

Example	*The /əʊ/ vowel sound:*	*The 'Rolling Stones'*
		an 'own goal'
		'Coca Cola'
	The /ɒ/ vowel sound:	*a 'sausage dog'*
		'lost property office'
		a 'pot of coffee'

Follow-up

Ask students use the items to invent tongue twisters.

5.7 You're simply the best!

Level Elementary +

Time 45 minutes

Aims To practise comparative and superlative forms.

Preparation

1 Find and download a few superlative images.

Example
- Robert Pershing Wadlow: *the tallest man in medical history* (see image on page 107)
- Mount Everest: *the highest mountain in the world*
- *the richest man in the world* (use an online encyclopaedia to find out who it is)
- the blue whale: *the biggest animal that has ever lived on our planet*
- the Nile: *the longest river in the world*
- the crawl: *the fastest swimming stroke*
- the butterfly: *the most difficult swimming stroke*
- poster for: *the most expensive film ever made* (use an online encyclopaedia to find out what it is)
- Mercury: *the closest planet to the sun*
- Neptune: *the furthest planet from the sun* (Pluto was relegated to the status of 'dwarf planet' by the International Astronomical Union in August 2006).

2 Arrange the images as a slide show (see Appendix 3, page 131) and decide upon a display medium (computer, projector, interactive whiteboard, etc).

3 Find a picture of Tina Turner and, if possible, get hold of her song 'The Best' (often known as 'Simply the Best'). The music and video can be found online at video-sharing sites.

Procedure

1 Show students the picture of Tina Turner and ask them what they know about her. Ask if they can name (or sing) any of her songs.

2 Play 'Simply the Best' and ask students if they know the words to the best-known part of the chorus ('You're simply the best, better than all the rest').

3 Draw a numbered grid on the board that corresponds to this line of the song. Each line should represent an individual word:

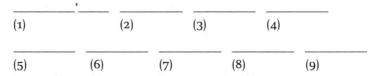

4 Ask students to listen to the song line again and then ask them to suggest whole words—one at a time—that fit on to the grid (you may have to give them a word or two to start them off). For each suggested word, students should also give you the numbered position on to which it should be placed. Write correct answers on the grid.

5 Each time a student gives an incorrect answer (this will be either an incorrect word or an incorrect position), add an extra part to the 'hangman' diagram as shown below. Make a note of all incorrect guesses on the board so that students don't repeat them.

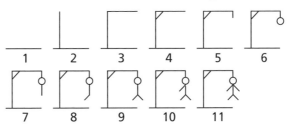

6 Play the important part of the song as many times as your students want to hear it. Students win if they successfully manage to identify the whole line before making 11 incorrect guesses.

7 Once the song line has been identified, drill it and ask everyone write it down.

8 Tell students that you are going to show them a superlative slide show. Show them the images one by one and in each case ask them to tell you what they see. In some cases they should be able to identify the superlative aspect in the picture and in some cases you will have to tell them yourself. For each image, ask students to write a sentence which contains the target language.

Example *Robert Pershing Wadlow is the tallest man in medical history.*
The butterfly is the most difficult swimming stroke.
The blue whale is the biggest animal that has ever lived on our planet.

9 Ask students to close their books. Repeat the slide show and for each image, see if they can recall the corresponding superlative sentence from memory. Drill these.

10 Repeat the slide show once more and for each image, ask your students what Tina Turner would sing.

Example *You're simply the furthest planet from the sun, further than all the rest.*
You're simply the longest river in the world, longer than all the rest.
You're simply the easiest swimming stroke, easier than all the rest.

11 Ask students to write down each sentence. This can be followed by encouraging them to sing or chant the lines to the melody and/or rhythm of Tina Turner's song. Note, however, that in most cases, the new words ('furthest planet from the sun', etc.) will have to be 'squashed together' if they are to fit.

Follow-up

Repeat this drill at later dates whenever the target language needs to be readdressed.

Comment

See Introduction, page 5 for more information about Robert Pershing Wadlow.

5.8 Irregular verb family book covers

Level   Pre-intermediate +

Time   60 minutes

Aims   To learn vocabulary from book covers.

Preparation

1   Online book stores (see Appendix 7g, page 134) are a valuable source of images for English teachers. The ability to find books (and DVDs) with specific words in the title allows us to create useful slide shows of covers for students. Consider the following titles:

- *Frozen in time*
- *I froze my mother*
- *Woken furies*
- *The wife he chose*
- *The chosen one*
- *How to speak dog*
- *God spoke to me*
- *My first spoken words*
- *Wake up and change your life*
- *I woke up one day and I was 40*
- *Why don't penguins' feet freeze?*
- *How to choose the sex of your baby*
- *First, break all the rules*
- *The man who broke Napoleon's codes*
- *I can mend your broken heart*
- *How to steal the crown jewels*
- *Aliens stole my underpants*
- *Inside the world of stolen art.*

These titles would be very useful for teaching the different forms of an irregular verb family: *speak-spoke-spoken, choose-chose-chosen, freeze-froze-frozen,* etc. Images of book covers like these can be found by running searches on individual words (*stole, break, woken,* etc.) at an online book store and browsing through the results that are obtained.

2   Whenever you find a good book cover, click on 'see larger image' and then save it on to your hard drive.

3   Arrange the images as a slide show (see Appendix 3, page 131) and decide how you are going to display it in class.

4   Create a worksheet that lists all the book titles.

5   Create a second worksheet that lists the book genres in random order (this is optional). This second worksheet should give basic information such as: 'A popular science book', 'a self-help book', 'a crime thriller', 'a children's book of poems', 'a men's health guide', 'a romantic novel', etc.

Procedure

1 Give your students the first worksheet and ask if they can work out what the pieces of language are (i.e. book titles).

2 Elicit types of books from your students and write terms on the board such as 'a self-help book', 'a novel', 'fiction', 'non-fiction', 'a poetry book', etc.

3 Ask students to work together (as a whole class, in groups, or in pairs) to come to a consensus decision about each title and decide what type of book it is. This could be a time-consuming task, so set a time limit (ten minutes for example). If you prepared a worksheet containing descriptions, give these out and ask students to match them with the titles.

4 Let students share and compare their answers.

5 Show students the slide show. Aspects of image, design, colour, graphics, font, and additional text will usually allow students to see the genre of the books and allow them to correct their work.

6 Go over the slide show a second time and ask students to translate all of the titles into their own language.

7 Ask students to pair up and attempt to translate the titles back into English.

8 Play the slide show a third time to allow students to correct their work.

9 Ask your students to the language point in the slide show. In this case it would be the six verbs with similar pronunciation of the past and past participle forms.

Variation 1

Similar activities can be created with DVD covers from online music and film stores.

Variation 2

An online book or music store can be regarded as a learner-friendly corpus. By typing words or phrases into the search window, there is a huge range of language that be found.

Example
- books or DVDs with either 'remember' or 'remind' in the title
- books or DVDs with either 'can' or 'could' in the title
- books or DVDs with either 'could have', 'should have', or 'would have' in the title
- books or DVDs with 'used to' in the title
- book or DVD titles containing present perfect continuous structures (find these by typing 'been' into the search window).

Variation 3

After seeing a slide show of covers, give students a title and ask them to recall and describe the cover from memory. Alternatively, you can describe covers and ask students to identify the title.

Comments

1   Book and film covers combine words with pictures and this may enhance a learner's experience of a target structure or piece of vocabulary. And since the language of book and film titles is diverse, online stores can prove to be a very effective tool for both teachers and learners alike.

2   In many cases, the titles of books and films are easy for a learner to understand, even when they contain language that has never been met or studied. This comes down to the fact that they are short, potentially autonomous in meaning, and visually supported.

3   When choosing images for students, it is good to look for covers that may be appreciated even when the book has not been read or the film has not been seen. Although we may not know specifically what the title refers to, elements of colour, design, image, graphics, and font will allow the imagination to take over and come to its own decision.

6

Student-generated flashcards

Drawing can be an extremely effective technique for the language classroom. The process of converting a piece of target language into a tangible image allows the learner to gain experience of it, and provides the teacher with a means of revisiting it at later dates. Although it is often associated with younger students, drawing is an activity that can be considered for language learners of all ages. It is certainly true that some adults and teenagers may feel a little awkward about doing so. But it is also true that persuading such students to draw is often much easier than persuading them to sing. In any case, a couple of good drawing activities will usually convince the reluctant artists that the process can be highly beneficial to their learning.

The activities in this chapter use sets of paper-based picture flashcards which are drawn by students themselves. Flashcards should be:

- small (to save paper)
- quick (time-consuming works of art should be discouraged)
- black and white (students can use their own pencils or pens to draw)
- two-sided (the picture should appear on one side and the text label on the other).

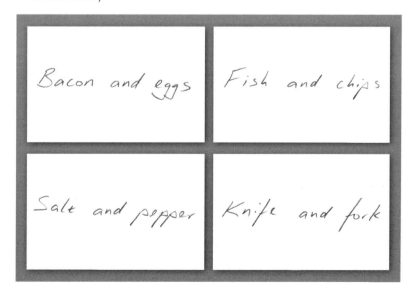

Basic method for making flashcards

Preparation

1 Compile a list of vocabulary items that you would like your students to draw and learn. The list may be as simple or complex as you like. A food and drink theme, for example, could include any of the following:

Example
a chicken sandwich
an aubergine and a courgette
a bunch of grapes
a loaf of bread
a tin of tuna fish
a cup of coffee

a 4-season pizza
a packet of chocolate biscuits
a piece of cake
a glass of freshly squeezed orange juice
a bottle of olive oil
a coffee cup

2 Prepare the flashcards by tearing up sheets of paper into equal-sized rectangles.

3 Write the items of vocabulary on to the blank cards. Write lightly with a pencil so that the text cannot be seen through the other side. This would allow students to cheat in activities such as 'Get rid of your cards' (Activity 6.5).

Procedure

1 Spread all the labelled pieces of paper over a table or on the floor, text-side-up, and invite students to look at them. Elicit definitions whenever possible and drill pronunciation whenever necessary. Clarify any words or items that students do not know (draw your own pictures on the board, translate into students' own language, provide bilingual dictionaries, etc.).

2 Tell students that they are going to draw the vocabulary items on the non-text sides of the pieces of paper. Ask students to draw quickly and tell them that the idea is not to create masterpieces. Demonstrate with an example of your own.

3 Allow everyone to select something that they feel comfortable with drawing. As soon as a student finishes a drawing he or she should choose another one to do. You may find that some students make several flashcards while others only make one.

4 Collect in all the flashcards and use the pictures to elicit, drill, and teach the language on the reverse sides.

5 Keep flashcards for revision games and activities at later dates.

Ad hoc flashcards

Flashcards can be created at any time in response to the language that arises in the classroom. For example, any of the following speaking tasks could result in a good number of new words and items being written on the board:

- Tell a partner everything you have eaten today.
- Tell a partner everything you ate last night.
- Tell a partner what your ideal meal would be.
- Tell a partner what food you don't like.
- Tell a partner what food you miss living away from home/what food you would miss if you lived away from home.
- Tell a partner all the ingredients, utensils, and appliances you need to make your favourite recipe.

In such cases, capture new language by handing out blank flashcards (always have a pile of these at hand) and asking students to draw it. Text labels can be added later and a flashcard bank can be built up over time (see Appendix 12, page 137).

Flashcard themes

When selecting themes for picture flashcards, the possibilities are endless. Here are a few ideas in no particular order.

Basic vocabulary themes

- food, animals, jobs, clothes, etc.
- things you find in the classroom, office, street, etc.

Images for remembering confusing words

- an angry kangaroo and a hungry monkey
- a photographer taking a photograph of a photographic model
- a cook cooking chicken in the kitchen (see picture A, page 116)

Questions

- What time did you get up this morning?
- How many coffees do you drink in a day?
- Have you got any children?

Idioms and sayings

- Too many cooks spoil the broth.
- to throw out the baby with the bath water
- to keep an eye out for someone (see picture B, page 116)

A Picture by Roser

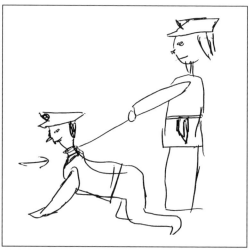

B Picture by Sara

C Picture by Gemma

D Picture by Àngels

E Picture by Coral

F Picture by Oscar

Phrases or sentences containing passive structures

- a football player being sent off
- a rude customer being asked to leave
- a criminal being released on bail

Make, do, or have collocations

- making the bed
- doing a runner from a restaurant (see picture C opposite)
- having an argument

Student mistakes

- I am scared of The Beatles. (should have been 'scared of beetles')
- They stole my grandmother. (should have been 'robbed my grandmother')
- My flat has a small chicken. (should have been 'a small kitchen')
- He works as a dog. (should have been 'like a dog') (see picture D opposite)

Things students say in free conversation

- If my English was as good as my cooking, I would be happy. (see picture E opposite)
- When I was on holiday, I got chased by bees. (see picture F opposite)

These can be utterances that were either praiseworthy or needed correction.

6.1 Who drew what?

Level Beginner +

Time 15 minutes

Aims To recall the language on the back of flashcards. To practise structures containing possessive pronouns.

Preparation

Obtain a set of student flashcards using the basic method set out on page 114 and put them in a box.

Procedure

1 Write the following language on the board, for students to copy.

Is this yours?	Yes, it's mine. No, I don't know whose it is. No, (I think) it's Felipe's.
What do you think it is?	I've got no idea. I think it's a ... It looks like a ...

2 Ask students to form a circle around you if possible.

3 Take a flashcard out of the box and show it to your class. Turn to a random student and ask the first question (*Is this yours?*). Use the language on the board to elicit a suitable response. Repeat the question with different students until the artist has been identified.

4 Turn to a different student (i.e. not the artist) and ask the second question in the box (*What do you think it is?*). Again, use the language on the board to elicit a suitable response. Repeat the question two or three times with different students before asking the artist to confirm what he or she has drawn. In case of confusion, turn the flashcard around to reveal the text side.

5 Continue this process with a few more flashcards.

6 Once students have become familiar with the routine, invite individuals to ask the questions by passing them the flashcard box.

Comments

The success of this activity depends on students speaking only when asked questions. For this reason, students should be discouraged from shouting out when others are speaking.

Variation

Learners often confuse the question *Whose is this?* with *Who is this?* This activity can be a good opportunity to practise these two forms especially when the flashcards contain pictures of people.

6.2 Criminals and couch potatoes

Level Elementary +

Time 60 minutes

Aims To practise pronunciation of the third person singular *-s*

Preparation

1 Refer to the basic flashcard preparation method (see page 114) to prepare 12 blank flashcards with the following text labels:

- a baby sitter
- a detective
- a philosopher
- a ski instructor
- a couch potato
- a hooligan
- a pilot
- a social butterfly
- a criminal
- an optimist
- a postman
- a vandal

2 Make a copy of worksheet 6.2 on page 120 for each student.

Procedure

1 Write the following verbs on the board:

- break
- damage
- have
- teach
- catch
- deliver
- look after
- think
- cause
- fly
- see
- watch

Photocopiable © Oxford University Press

Worksheet 6.2

Use the verbs on the board (in third person singular form) to complete the following sentences:

1 A babysitter is a person who _____ your children when you go out.

2 A couch potato is a person who _____ too much TV.

3 A criminal is a person who _____ the law.

4 A detective is a person who _____ criminals.

5 A hooligan is a person who _____ trouble at football matches.

6 A philosopher is a person who _____ about the meaning of life.

7 A pilot is a person who _____ planes.

8 A postman is a person who _____ letters.

9 A ski instructor is a person who _____ skiing.

10 A social butterfly is a person who _____ a lot of friends.

11 A vandal is a person who _____ public property.

12 An optimist is a person who _____ a glass as half full.

Photocopiable © Oxford University Press

2 Demonstrate to students that when a third person singular verb or a plural noun ends in -s, there are three possible ways in which the ending can be produced:

1 Ends in /s/	2 Ends in /z/	3 Ends in /ɪz/
Grape	Banana	Orange
Grapes	Bananas	Oranges

3 Ask students to listen to your pronunciation of the third person singular forms of the verbs on the board and in each case ask them to decide which sound they hear at the end.

Example Teacher: *I break but he or she breaks.*
Student: *Ending 1.*
Teacher: *I catch but he or she catches.*
Student: *Ending 3.*

Answer:
/s/ breaks, thinks, looks after
/z/ delivers, flies, has, sees
/ɪz/ catches, causes, damages, teaches, watches

(See Comment on page 122 for a discussion of the pronunciation rule.)

4 Drill pronunciation of these verb forms.

5 Show your students the text-sides of the blank 'people' flashcards one at a time and in each case try to elicit definitions. Ask students to describe what the people do rather than offer you a direct translation to their own language and encourage them to use the verbs on the board whenever possible.

Example *Teacher: What is a pilot?*
Student: A person who flies planes.

Encourage students to make guesses for the ones they don't know (*couch potato* and *social butterfly* for example).

6 Lay the blank flashcards on a table or on the floor, text-side-up, and ask students to provide the pictures as outlined in the basic flashcard procedure (see page 114). Students can be imaginative for the ones they don't know.

7 Collect in all the cards and identify who drew what.

8 Give out copies of Worksheet 6.2 and ask students to complete it using the verbs on the board.

9 Let students compare their answers with each other before feedback and drilling.

Answers:

1 A babysitter is a person who **looks after** your children when you go out.
2 A couch potato is a person who **watches** too much TV.
3 A criminal is a person who **breaks** the law.
4 A detective is a person who **catches** criminals.
5 A hooligan is a person who **causes** trouble at football matches.
6 A philosopher is a person who **thinks** about the meaning of life.
7 A pilot is a person who **flies** planes.
8 A postman is a person who **delivers** letters.
9 A ski instructor is a person who **teaches** skiing.
10 A social butterfly is a person who **has** a lot of friends.
11 A vandal is a person who **damages** public property.
12 An optimist is a person who **sees** a glass as half full.

10 Ask students to turn over their worksheets. Use the flashcards to elicit and drill the 12 sentences.

Variation

By changing the word *person* to *people*, certain features of grammar also change.

• A postman is a person who delivers letters.
• Postmen are people who deliver letters.

When using the flashcards to drill the sentences, toss a coin and ask students to use the 'person' version if it lands on heads and the 'people' version if it lands on tails.

Comment

Students may be unable to distinguish between third person singular forms that end in /s/ (*forgets*) and those that end in /z/ (*forgives*). If this is the case, teachers would be advised not to dwell on this point but to reassure students that the /s/ or /z/ sound will generally be produced naturally as a result of the sound that precedes it. More importantly, teachers may decide to draw attention to verbs that end in /ʃ/, /tʃ/, /z/, /s/, and /dʒ/ as their third person singular forms will require the production of an additional syllable.

Verb	Syllables	3rd person sing. form	Syllables
Wash /ʃ/	O	Washes	Oo
Match /tʃ/	O	Matches	Oo
Lose /z/	O	Loses	Oo
Dress /s/	O	Dresses	Oo
Judge /dʒ/	O	Judges	Oo

(Note O = strong syllable, o = weak syllable)

6.3 Quiz

Level Elementary +

Time 45 minutes

Aims To reconstruct sentences and noun phrases.

Preparation

Use the basic method on page 114 to obtain a few student-generated flashcards for noun phrases containing *-ing* forms of verbs. These could have a preposition or phrasal verb theme:

- a queue of people waiting for a bus
- a man listening to jazz
- a woman trying on a new dress
- a plane taking off
- a couple looking at paintings in a gallery
- a frog turning into a good-looking prince
- a little girl looking up rude words in the dictionary
- a man on a desert island thinking about his wife (see below left)
- two people making up after falling out (see below right).

Drawing by Miquel

Drawing by Àngels

Procedure

1 Show students one of the flashcards and ask them what it is. Help with the language if necessary and write the question and answer on the board.

Example *What is this?*
A woman trying on a new dress.

2 After repeating this with a few more flashcards, return to the first one you showed and ask what is happening. This is a different question than before and will require an answer that is a sentence in the present continuous rather than a noun phrase. Again, help with the language if necessary and write the question and answer on the board.

Example *What is happening?*
A woman is trying on a new dress.

3 Ask students if they can see the difference between the two answers. If they have any doubts, ask them to translate the structures into their own language. This will generally help since this aspect of grammar is consistent in all languages.

4 Put students into pairs or groups and tell them that they are going to have a quiz. Show a flashcard and ask either of the questions mentioned above:

- *What is this?*
- *What is happening?*

Rather than shouting out the answers, ask each pair or group to confer and write down the full corresponding noun phrase or present continuous sentence. Importantly, keep a note of the flashcards you have shown and the questions you have asked.

5 At the end of the quiz, take in everyone's answer sheets. Lay these out in front of you and go over the questions one by one (referring to the flashcards as you do so) and mark students' answers as you progress through them. In each case, drill pronunciation of the target language.

6 Award a point for every well-constructed sentence or noun phrase and find out which pair or group is the winner.

Variation

Rather than writing down answers, students can be asked to say what they see and points can be awarded accordingly. This works best for smaller groups since only one person can speak at a time.

Comment

Students may demonstrate a lack of noun phrase awareness when they attempt to construct or reconstruct larger texts.

Example *In the photograph we see a young Chinese photographer taking a photo of his friend Mike.* (See Activity 1.1.)

Activities that draw attention to noun phrases may help students to self-correct at times like these.

6.4 Galleries

Level Pre-intermediate +

Time 30 minutes

Aims To reconstruct sentences or phrases.

Preparation

For this activity, you will need to think of a few sentences or phrases that contain a grammatical structure that you want to teach. For example, if you wanted to use the structure, *'waiting for something to happen'*, refer to the basic flashcard preparation method (see page 114) to create flashcards with the following text labels:

- waiting for the phone to ring
- waiting for the last customers to leave
- waiting for a girl like you to come into my life
- waiting for the referee to blow the final whistle
- waiting for the band to come on
- waiting for the kettle to boil
- waiting for the bell to ring (see below)
- waiting for the rain to stop (see below).

Drawing by Roser   Drawing by Àngels

Procedure

1 Once students have finished drawing their flashcards, put them up around the classroom walls and label them numerically.

2 Ask students to browse the gallery, look at the work on display, and write down what they think each picture represents.

3 Ask everyone to compare their answers in pairs.

4 Finally ask the artists to recall the language and refer to the text labels on the reverse sides of the flashcards to clarify.

Variation 1

If you decide to use the 'waiting for something to happen' structure outlined in this activity, it could be introduced by covering up the left hand side of the photograph used in Activity 3.9 and asking students to guess what the waiter is waiting for (i.e. the last customers to leave).

Variation 2

Write the following questions on the board.

- *If you could be any animal, what animal would you be?*
- *If you could have dinner with anyone in the world (dead or alive), who would you choose?*
- *What would you do if you could be president/prime minister for the day?*
- *What would you do if you could turn back time?*
- *If you won a fortune, what would you do with the money?*

Ask students to choose one question and write their full answer on a piece of paper. Offer linguistic help as they do so and then ask them to draw their answers on the reverse sides and write their names. Create a picture gallery as before and ask everyone to walk around and attempt to guess each other's conditional structures from their drawings.

Variation 3

Select a number of example sentences from your students' text book or exercise book. They should be based around a language point that you are currently teaching (the modal verb *will*, for example).

- *She washed the dishes quickly.*
- *She sings very loudly.*
- *He looked suspiciously at everyone that got off the plane.* (see below)

Dictate these examples to your students and let them pair up to check what they have written. Ask for volunteers to draw sentences and give out blank pieces of paper accordingly. Put the pictures up around the classroom walls as before and ask students to browse the gallery to see if they can recall and write down the sentences from memory.

Drawing by Ishah

6.5 Get rid of your cards

Level All levels

Time 20 minutes

Aims To revise language on flashcards.

Preparation

Select about 20 flashcards that you wish to revise and make photocopies so that each group has its own set. Note that it will be necessary to add the text labels after photocopying.

Procedure

1 Show your students all the flashcards that are going to be used and recap the language.

2 Pair up students or put them into groups of three or four. Give each group a set of flashcards and ask them to deal them out as equally as possible between each other.

3 Each player takes it in turn to put down a card in the middle of the table, picture-side-up, and say what it is. If a player looks at the language side of the card while doing so, this is cheating! In fact it is worthwhile pointing out to your students that the cards must be held picture-side up at all times in order to avoid cheating.

4 If a player produces the language correctly, the card stays down. If the player makes a mistake, they have to pick up all the cards that have already been put down on the pile. The first player to put down all of his or her cards is the winner. Players may use the back of the cards (i.e. the text sides) for arbitration.

5 While your students are playing this game, go around the class making sure that they are producing the language correctly.

Variation

There are two ways of playing 'Get rid of your cards'. In the first version, players are allowed to look at all the cards in their hand before deciding which one to put down on the table. This means that they may decide to play the easy ones first and, as a result, the difficult ones receive less attention. In order to get around this, players can be made to put down cards 'blind'. In other words, they must always put down the first flashcard in their hand whatever it is.

6.6 Stepping stones

Level All levels

Time 20 minutes

Aims To revise language on flashcards.

Preparation

Select about 16 flashcards that you wish to revise.

Procedure

1 Lay out the flashcards picture-side-up in a line on a table or on the floor. These are the stepping stones. Give all players pieces or markers and have them place these at the start of the line.

Line of flashcards

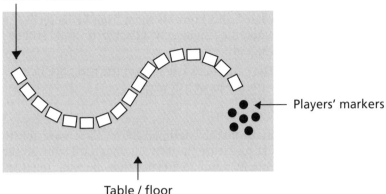

Table / floor

Players' markers

2 Instead of a dice, players throw a coin. If it lands on 'heads', the player's piece is moved up one stepping stone and if it lands on tails, it is moved up two. After each throw, the player must pronounce the corresponding language for the flashcard stepping stone that he or she lands on.

3 If the player produces the language of the flashcard correctly, he or she is allowed to move up one more stepping stone before play is passed to the next person. The text on the back of the flashcards can be referred to in the case of disputes.

4 As the teacher, you should swap around the positions of the stepping stones regularly throughout this game so that play does not focus on the same flashcards. For this reason, ask students to place their markers beside the stepping stones rather than on top of them.

5 The first player to reach the other side of the stepping stones is the winner.

6.7 Fishing

Level All levels

Time 20 minutes

Aims To revise language on flashcards.

Preparation

Select about 16 flashcards that you wish to revise.

Procedure

1 Spread all the flashcards picture-side-up on the table or on the floor. This is the sea.

2 Players take it in turn to 'catch a fish'. In order to do this they should pick up a flashcard and say what it is. A correct answer allows the player to keep the fish and an incorrect one results in it being passed to the teacher. Let players refer to the text on the back of the flashcards to settle disputes.

3 The teacher should return fish to the sea after a few shots have passed (this prevents them from being picked up straight away when the language of a flashcard would still be ringing in students' ears).

4 The game ends when all of the fish have been caught. The player with the most fish wins.

Variation

In the method outlined above, players are able to focus on the easy fish and leave the difficult ones until later. To get around this, you should nominate the fish that you want the first player to catch by pointing to it. After that player's turn, he or she should then nominate another fish for the next player and so on. When played in this way, fish can be returned directly to the sea rather than being passed to the teacher following incorrect answers.

Appendix

1 Image search engine guide

The Internet itself is the largest repository of images the world has ever seen. Image search engines allow us to conduct searches using key words or phrases to find exactly what we are looking for.

Procedure

1 Go to any standard internet search engine such as:

- www.google.com
- www.search.yahoo.com
- www.altavista.com
- www.live.com
- www.picsearch.com.

2 At each site, you will see the word 'Images' somewhere above the search window. Click on it and you will be taken to the corresponding image search engine.

3 Type a word or phrase into the search window corresponding to what you are looking for and click on the *search* or *find* button. For example:

Desired image	Text to type into search window
a film poster (see Activity 3.7)	[The name of the film]
a picture of Damien Hirst's 'The physical impossibility of death in the mind of someone living' (see Activity 3.10)	Hirst physical impossibility
a flag being flown at half mast (see Activity 4.9)	flag half mast
the Japanese flag (see Activity 4.9)	Japan flag
Bart Simpson making a prank phone call (see Activity 4.10)	Bart prank call
a photograph of an athlete competing in the long jump (see Activity 5.5)	long jump
someone eating breakfast in bed (see Activity 5.6)	breakfast in bed

4 In each case, you will be presented with a page of thumbnail (miniature) images. Images will vary in degree of relevancy: Some will be related to what you are looking for and others won't. Scroll through the pages until you find an image that you like.

5 You will be able to see an image in its full size. For most image search engines, you will be given this option when you click on a thumbnail. Find one of good size and quality.

6 To save an image on a PC, right click on it (in full size) and choose 'Save image as …'. This will give you the option to save it to your hard disk, memory stick, etc. Images can then be printed off and laminated or arranged on a computer as a slide show (see Appendix 3). For Macs, image save options are accessed by pressing control and clicking the mouse while the cursor is over an image.

7 Different search engines offer different search options. Most of them, for example, will allow you to search exclusively for black and white images. Look out for 'Search Options' functions.

Note that when using search engines, it can take time and patience to find exactly what you are looking for. The more you use a search engine (text or image), the more you will develop a 'sense' for it.

Using image searches in class

In order to avoid unfortunate surprises in the classroom, you must make sure that the image search engine filter system is on. This is a straightforward process. For example, if you are using Google image search, click on 'Preferences' and scroll down the page until you see 'SafeSearch Filtering'. Select 'Use strict filtering', scroll back to the top of the page, and click 'Save Preferences'.

2 Blogs and photo sharing sites

Images used in the classroom (including scanned student drawings), can be uploaded on to a class webpage along with the texts that accompany them. This can motivate and encourage students to revisit and revise language. A class webpage could be a blog, a page on a social networking site, a page on a photo sharing site, etc. The following is a very small sample of some of the sites that allow such possibilities:

- www.blogger.com (a popular blogging site)
- www.wordpress.com (another popular blogging site)
- www.facebook.com (a popular networking site)
- www.spaces.live.com ('Windows Live Spaces'—Microsoft's user-friendly blogging/networking site)
- www.flickr.com (see below)

Any text that is used or created in class in association with an image can be uploaded beside it. This could include any of the following:

- Texts used in conjunction with mental image dictations, standard dictations, or running dictations (see Chapter 1)
- Texts used in conjunction with reading activities (see Activities 2.2 and 2.5, for example)

- Student captions (see Activities 3.3, 3.4, and 3.10, for example)
- Student compositions (see Activities 3.5–3.9, for example)

Photo-sharing sites

A photo sharing site such as Flickr (www.flickr.com) or Fotolog (www.fotolog.com) allows users to create and share their own online photograph albums. Uploaded images can be accompanied by text and arranged into sets. Such sites are useful for uploading class photographs (see Activity 4.13, for example) and making contact with other users (see Activity 4.17, Variation 2, for example). Furthermore, users can comment on each other's pictures.

Flickr is particularly notable for its communities or 'groups' that share similar interests (see Activity 4.5). In addition, photographs that are uploaded may be 'text labelled'. This is a very useful feature that allows the user to add captions on to different parts of the picture that remain invisible until the mouse cursor is moved over them.

3 Digital slide shows

- PCs and Macs come equipped with image organizers or other standard applications (Windows Picture and Fax Viewer or Preview, for example) which allow users to create sets of images (including scanned student-generated flashcards) and display them as onscreen slide shows in class.
- Photo-sharing sites (see Appendix 2) and free image organizers such as Picasa (see Appendix 4) can be used to create online slide shows. The fact that such applications allow images to be accompanied by pieces of text means that teachers can put entire series of labelled flash images (see Chapter 5) online and send out the link to students.
- PowerPoint can also be used to create and display slide shows.
- Series of images can be converted into Adobe PDF files which can be sent to students. The same can be done with PowerPoint presentations.
- Video-editing software such as Windows Movie Maker or Final Cut Express 4 (for PCs and Macs respectively) can be used to convert slide shows into video clips. These in turn can be uploaded on to video-sharing sites such as www.youtube.com.

4 Image organizers

For the technologically minded teacher, a good image organizer can be an invaluable asset. For example:

- Picasa (can be downloaded free at www.picasa.google.com)
- Aperture 2 (for Macs)

Such applications can be used to:

- quickly find pictures that you have previously downloaded (assuming that they have been labelled appropriately)
- create slide shows which can be stored on your computer (see Appendix 3)

- create online slide shows (see Appendix 3)
- crop images
- zoom in and out of images
- convert colour images into black and white (see Activity 4.2, Variation)
- create collages (of scanned student-generated flashcards for example)
- label images with pieces of text.

5 Cover ups

Microsoft Paint (standard with PCs) and similar applications can be used to cover up parts of images (see Activity 4.13, Follow-up 1, for example).

Procedure

1 Duplicate an image so that you can deface one and keep the original intact (this can be done with copy and paste functions).

2 Open the duplicated image with Microsoft Paint. This can be done by right clicking on the image and selecting 'Open with'.

3 Select the paint brush tool on the left hand side of the screen.

4 Scribble around the part of the picture that you want to hide. Do this by holding down the left mouse button while you move the cursor around.

5 When you are happy with your result, save the image and close it.

This technique can be very effective for concealing key pieces of text on images of book and DVD covers (see Activity 5.8). For Macs, applications such as Adobe Illustrator can be used for this purpose.

6 Screen captures

A screen capture (sometimes screenshot or screen dump) is effectively a 'photograph' taken by your computer to record the display that appears on its screen. Screen captures can be used for any of the following:

- to obtain film stills (see Activity 4.10)
- to prepare 'shots' of image search results to show to learners when there is no online access in class (see Variation 1 of Activity 5.1)

Procedure

1 Set up your computer screen or monitor with the display you want to capture. For example, if you want a film still, play the DVD on your computer and pause it at the exact moment that you want to capture.

2 PC users: Look for the 'Print Screen' button near the top right hand side of your keypad and press it once. Mac users: Hold down Apple and shift together and press 4 (the number key).

3 For PC users, open Microsoft Paint (see Appendix 5), paste the screen capture on to the screen (Ctrl + V), then save the image.

4 For Mac users, the screen capture will automatically be saved as an image file on your desktop.

7 Websites

The following is a list of image websites, many of which have been referred to in activities throughout the book.

a Maps and online location finders
- Google Earth: www.earth.google.com (a versatile site that can be used for anything from guessing the country from above to exploring unfamiliar cities at ground level)
- Google maps: www.maps.google.com (for looking at plans of cities)
- Google maps pedometer: www.gmap-pedometer.com (as Google maps but allows users to plan routes)

b Guinness World Records: www.guinnessworldrecords.com (pictures of record breakers). See Activity 4.3.

c Film sites
- Many films have their own websites which contain images and stills (see http://chocolatefactorymovie.warnerbros.com, for example)
- Internet Movie Database: www.imdb.com (for film posters)

d Art websites
- National galleries usually have websites where images of exhibited pieces as well as information about them can be obtained (see www.tate.org.uk, for example)
- Museum of bad art: www.museumofbadart.org (full of tasteless gems)
- BBC (British Broadcasting Corporation: public service broadcasting company): www.bbc.co.uk/arts/art (a good selection of galleries)
- The Guardian: Go to 'In pictures' at www.guardian.co.uk/artanddesign for a range of online galleries.

e Online news images
- Online newspapers often have daily slide shows of photographs from around the world (see for example 'In pictures' at www.guardian.co.uk for a great range of diverse images)
- BBC 'On this day': www.news.bbc.co.uk/onthisday (recreated news stories for famous events, searchable by date).

f Photography and other image competitions (see Activity 4.17)
- London international awards: www.liaawards.com (set up to award exceptional creative work in advertising, design, and digital media. Previous years' winners and finalists can be seen on the website.)
- Worth1000: www.worth1000.com ('Photoshop contest website' where contestants creatively manipulate images, post them on to the site, and allow viewers to vote for their favourites)

- Wildlife photographer of the year: www.nhm.ac.uk/wildphoto
- Wikimedia Commons Picture of the Year: http://commons.wikimedia.org/wiki/Commons:Picture_of_the_Year

g Amazon: www.amazon.co.uk (online book, music, and film store, good for images of book and DVD covers). See Activity 5.8.

h Video-sharing sites. (Please note that moving images may potentially be more shocking than non-moving images. Since there is usually no way of filtering searches on video-sharing sites, we strongly advise that teachers select appropriate clips before class rather than running live searches in front of students.)

- YouTube: www.youtube.com
- Teflclips: www.teflclips.com (a site dedicated to the use of video-sharing in language learning).

i Miscellaneous image sources and websites

- Adbusters: www.adbusters.com (anti-consumerist organization specializing in 'subverts'—spoofs or parodies of corporate or political advertisements in order to make a statement)
- Wikipedia: www.wikipedia.org (free online encyclopaedia, useful source for diverse images)
- Mugshots: www.mugshots.com (database of police booking photographs)
- The author's blog: www.jamiekeddie.com
- The Advertising Archives: www.advertisingarchives.co.uk (print and TV advertisements, cinema posters, ephemera)

8 Categories/sources of image

a Images of places: digital cameras, phone cameras, personal photographs, postcards, atlases, books (e.g. *Earth from Above*, see 'Further reading'), calendars, newspapers (especially international pages), magazines (e.g. *National Geographic*, see 'Further reading'), image search engines (see Appendix 1), websites (see Appendix 7a)

b Images of people: postcards, personal photographs, books, newspapers, magazines, image search engines (see Appendix 1)

c Art images: postcards, books (e.g. *The Art Book* or *The Photography Book*, see 'Further reading'), calendars, posters, photographs of local public art and graffiti, image search engines (see Appendix 1), art websites (see Appendix 7d)

d Film images (pictures of actors, directors, film stills, film posters, etc): Postcards, books, DVD boxes, catalogues of DVDs (often come inside new DVD boxes), screen captures (see Appendix 6), photographs of your TV screen, storyboards (often found in the extra features of DVDs), image search engines (see Appendix 1), film websites (see Appendix 7c), video-sharing sites (good for trailers and clips)

e News images: newspapers, books of historic news pictures (e.g. *100 Photographs that Changed the World*, see 'Further reading'), image search engines (see Appendix 1), websites (see Appendix 7e) f   Advertising images (magazines, newspapers, your own photographs of street adverts, photographs of TV screens, websites (see Appendices 7f and 7i)

9 Displaying images

- Ask students to gather around you and show them a picture in a book.
- Pass some images (laminated prints, postcards, etc.) round the class.
- Lay a selection of images on a table or on the floor so that everyone can see them.
- Put a selection of images on the classroom walls and create a gallery.
- Attach an image to the board (you can then add text around it). See image in Activity 3.5, for example.
- Use an overhead projector (excellent for covering up parts of the image and generating curiosity).
- Display images on a laptop (portability makes this method good for creating 'information gaps'. See Step 9 of Activity 4.4, for example.)
- Display images on a desktop and ask students to gather round the screen.
- Display images by projecting them from a computer on to a screen or interactive whiteboard.
- Display images electronically on a handheld device such as an MP3 player, mobile phone, or palmtop computer (excellent for very small groups and one-to-ones).
- Prepare a slide show (see Appendix 3).
- Email images to students before or after class.
- Upload images on to a class webpage and send the link to students before or after class.

10 Some more image sources

- bank notes, coins and stamps
- students' imaginations (for example, ask students to describe their dreams or the earliest images they can remember)
- second hand books (cut out and laminate images)
- cards (birthday, Christmas, anniversary, etc.)
- your television screen (take photographs of it)
- your computer screen (see Appendix 6)
- T-shirts that you wear to class
- camera phones
- your house, flat, or apartment (take photographs of it into class)
- your route to work (take photographs of any curious things you see)
- children's picture books (very engaging images, even for grown-ups)
- other classes (students will often be curious about their teacher's other classes. Introduce them via the pictures they draw but make sure you get permission first.)
- the classroom walls (have a good look at what is already up there)

- Sunday newspaper supplements (these can be particularly good)
- silly or fun pictures that people email to you
- expired wall calendars (12 good-sized, high quality images, all of them based around a common theme, make this resource one of the best for turning your classroom into a gallery)
- playing cards (themed, with a different picture on each card)

11 Twenty image basics

1. Show students an image and find out what they know about the subject. See Activities 2.4 and 4.1, for example.
2. Show students an image that has previously been used and ask them what they remember about it (good for revising language).
3. Dictate a picture (describe it to your students and ask them to draw it).
4. Use an image for a mental picture dictation. See Activity 1.1.
5. Ask students to work out what is in a picture by asking questions about it.
6. Make true or false statements about a picture and carry out an observation test. See Activity 1.4.
7. Use pictures to engage students with texts. See Activities 1.5, 2.2, or 2.5, for example.
8. Use images to give students homework. See Activity 2.4, for example.
9. Use a picture to test for photographic memory. See Activity 3.1.
10. Ask students to invent an explanation for a scenario in a picture. See Activities 3.1 and 3.8, for example.
11. Ask students to add thought or speech bubbles to the characters in a picture. See Activity 3.3.
12. Ask students to write captions or titles for pictures. See Activities 3.4 and 3.10, for example.
13. Ask students to put themselves in a picture and describe how they feel or what they would do in the situation.
14. Ask students work out the connection between two or more related images.
15. Ask students to create a fictitious connection between two unrelated images.
16. Flash an image at your learners and ask them to describe what they saw.
17. Double a picture. See Activity 4.3.
18. Chop up an image and ask students to hypothesize about the bigger picture. See Activity 4.4.
19. Zoom into an image and do the same.
20. Cover up parts of an image and ask students to guess what is happening.

12 Student-generated flashcard banks

Over time, a bank of Student-Generated Flashcards can be built up. Here are some ideas for storing and use:

- If you decide to store SGFs in a box, keep individual sets in separate, labelled envelopes.
- Laminate the best and most regularly used SGFs.
- Display SGFs in the classroom by hanging them up with clothes pegs on a 'washing line' (e.g. a piece of string). Make sure you change the display regularly.
- Scan SGFs and arrange them as a slide show. See Appendix 3. Students can also be sent PDF files of sets of SGFs (text labels can be included).
- Photocopy sets of SGFs (pictures sides). Give these to students and ask them to recall the language and label the pictures.

13 Ten commandments

1 During lesson planning, always think 'How can this activity be enhanced, improved, strengthened, and become more memorable to my students through the incorporation of image?'
2 Start to look at the images around you and your students and think, 'How can they be used to generate or teach language?'
3 Never download an article for your students in the printer-friendly version if this entails cutting off the images (printer friendly = student unfriendly).
4 Don't start off a class with a word or phrase written on the board when an image can easily be used instead.
5 Make good use of the classroom walls if you don't already do so.
6 Do not continually refer to your friends or family members without showing your students a photograph of them.
7 Do not use a song in class without showing your students a picture of the singer or band.
8 When using newspapers to create classroom activities, look at the images first.
9 Do the same when considering how to adapt activities in course books.
10 Always have a copy of an atlas or world map close at hand.

Further reading

100 Photographs that Changed the World. 2003. New York: Time Incorporated Home Entertainment.

Arthus-Bertrand, Y. 2005. *Earth from Above.* New York: Harry N. Abrams, Inc.

Ewen, S. 1990. Revised edn. *All Consuming Images: The Politics of Style in Contemporary Culture.* New York: Basic Books.

Fleckenstein, K. S. et al. 2002. New title edition. *Language and Image in the Reading-writing Classroom: Teaching Vision.* Mahwah, New Jersey: Lawrence Erlbaum Associates Inc.

Goldstein, B. 2008. *Working with Images.* Cambridge: Cambridge University Press.

Lester, P. M. 2002. 3rd edn. *Visual Communication: Images with Messages.* Florence, Kentucky: Wadsworth Publishing Co. Inc.

Maley, A. et al. 1981. *The Mind's Eye.* Cambridge: Cambridge University Press.

Kress, G. and T. van Leeuwen. 2006. (2nd edn.) *Reading images: The Grammar of Visual Design.* London: Routledge.

National Geographic Magazine. Tampa, Florida: National Geographic Society.

Puchta, H. et al. 2007. *Imagine That!: Mental Imagery in the EFL Classroom.* Cambridge: Cambridge University Press.

The Art Book. 1997. London: Phaidon Press.

The Photography Book. 2000. London: Phaidon Press.

Wright, A. 1989. *Pictures for Language Learning.* Cambridge: Cambridge University Press.

Wright, A. 1994 (2nd edn.) *1000 + Pictures for Teachers to Copy.* London: Nelson.

Index